Pushing Back

Pushing Back

WOMEN-OF-COLOR-LED
GRASSROOTS ACTIVISM
IN NEW YORK CITY

Ariella Rotramel

The University of Georgia Press

ATHENS

*Additional funding for this publication was provided
in part by Connecticut College Department of Gender,
Sexuality, and Intersectionality Studies*

© 2020 by the University of Georgia Press
Athens, Georgia 30602
www.ugapress.org
All rights reserved
Set in 10/13 Kepler Std by Kaelin Chappell Broaddus

Most University of Georgia Press titles are
available from popular e-book vendors.

Printed digitally

Library of Congress Cataloging-in-Publication Data

Names: Rotramel, Ariella, author.
Title: Pushing back : women of color-led grassroots activism
    in New York City / Ariella Rotramel.
Description: Athens : The University of Georgia Press, 2020. |
    Series: Since 1970 : histories of contemporary America |
    Includes bibliographical references and index.
Identifiers: LCCN 2019044538 (print) | LCCN 2019044539 (ebook)
    | ISBN 9780820356143 (hardback) | ISBN 9780820356662
    (paperback) | ISBN 9780820356136 (ebook)
Subjects: LCSH: Minority women—Political activity—New York
    (State)—New York. | Leadership in minority women—New York
    (State)—New York. | Women political activists—New York
    (State)—New York. | Social justice—New York (State)—New York.
Classification: LCC HQ1236.5.U6 R68 2020 (print) | LCC HQ1236.5.U6
    (ebook) | DDC 305.48/8—dc23
LC record available at https://lccn.loc.gov/2019044538
LC ebook record available at https://lccn.loc.gov/2019044539

CONTENTS

ILLUSTRATIONS

IMAGES

FIGURES

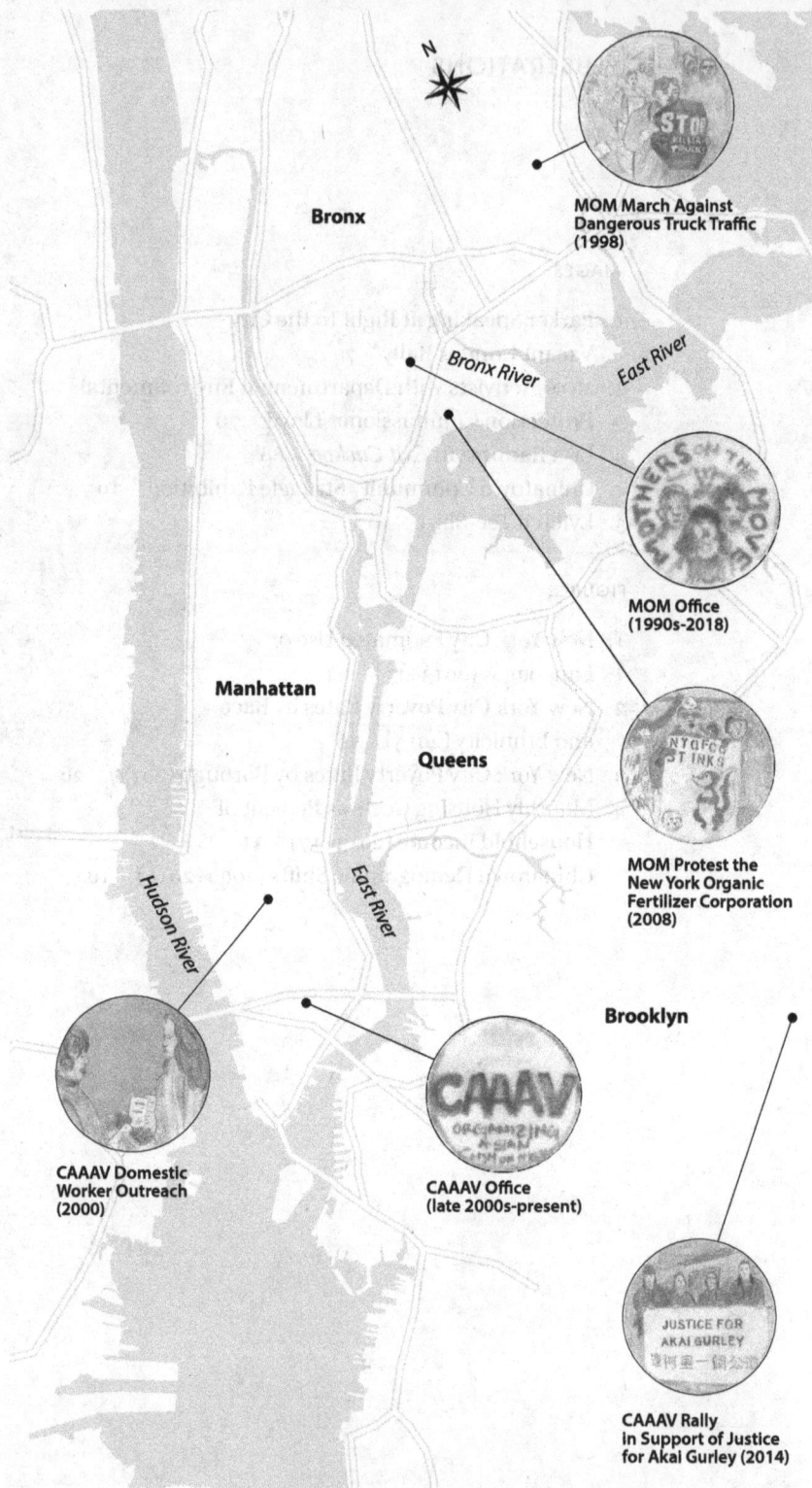

N

Bronx

Bronx River

East River

MOM March Against
Dangerous Truck Traffic
(1998)

MOM Office
(1990s-2018)

Manhattan

Queens

MOM Protest the
New York Organic
Fertilizer Corporation
(2008)

Hudson River

East River

Brooklyn

CAAAV Domestic
Worker Outreach
(2000)

CAAAV Office
(late 2000s-present)

JUSTICE FOR
AKAI GURLEY

CAAAV Rally
in Support of Justice
for Akai Gurley (2014)

MAP. Reference map by Andrea Wollensak. Illustrations by Ariella Rotramel.

Pushing Back

Pushing Back

INTRODUCTION

Situated Knowledge
and Action

> and when we speak we are afraid
> our words will not be heard
> nor welcomed
> but when we are silent
> we are still afraid
>
> **AUDRE LORDE, "A LITANY FOR SURVIVAL"**

In 2016, a coalition of Asian and Chinese organizations including Asian Americans United of Philadelphia, CAAAV: Organizing Asian Communities of New York City (formerly the Committee Against Anti-Asian Violence), the Chinatown Community for Equitable Development (CCED) of Los Angeles, and the San Francisco and Boston branches of the Chinese Progressive Association issued the following statement expressing anger at the lack of jail time for Peter Liang, a Chinese American New York Police Department officer who shot and killed Akai Gurley: "Our hunger for true justice, for a world where we all have a chance to thrive and grow old must be realized" (Rankin, "Asian-American Coalition"). Liang had been found guilty of killing the young Black man, a twenty-eight-year-old father who died in a Brooklyn public housing stairwell after being shot by the rookie officer. Asian activists came together to affirm the value of Black lives. They rejected calls from within the Asian community to hold Liang less accountable on the grounds of their shared identity as Asians. They disagreed with the argument that as white officers were never held accountable for their crimes by the justice system, the racism that was most concerning in this case was the potential anti-Asian racism against Liang. These groups mobilized out of explicitly racially identified groups, like CAAAV, and stood firm in their fundamental commitment to the prosecution of police for any instance of police brutality; in this case, it was another shooting of an unarmed Black man in New York. Belying claims that identity politics is divisive and overly simplistic, CAAAV and its allies chose to pursue an approach to identity politics that emphasizes a structural analysis of racist police violence. Rather than siding with Liang's family as Asians, they were consistent in their fight to support all communities facing racially motivated police violence.

CAAAV's complex approach to identity politics harkens back to the 1977 "Combahee River Collective Statement": "This focusing upon our own oppression is embodied in the concept of identity politics. We believe that the most profound and potentially the most radical politics come directly out of our own identity, as opposed to working to end somebody else's oppression" (19). As Black lesbian women, the members of the collective necessarily had to engage with their own identities and the oppressions tied to them. Identity politics is not only the province of leftist or progressive groups. Recently, its use by the right and by white supremacists has become a focal point of national and global conversations. The 2016 presidential election and its aftermath demonstrated the political power of U.S. white nationalism and what is seen as a resurgence of white identity politics. It is thus necessary to ask what identity politics offers social justice movements now. While groups like CAAAV and movements like Black Lives Matter and UndocuQueer have renewed a sense of possibility in the power of claiming a shared resistance to white supremacy and xenophobia, the public embrace of an unapologetic racist, xenophobic, and religious crusader whiteness in the United States, Europe, and Australia has raised questions about whether identity-based politics can produce just outcomes. Examining identity politics in practice through the case studies of two New York City immigrant- and women of color–led organizations, CAAAV and MOM, demonstrates the political necessity of a critical embrace of identity in this time of backlash. I use the term "women of color" as Loretta Ross does in recalling its roots in the 1977 National Women's Conference held in Houston, Texas. She says that it emerged out of "minority" women joining the Black Women's Agenda to address their concerns. "Woman of color" became "a solidarity definition, a commitment to work in collaboration with other oppressed women of color who have been 'minoritized'" (quoted in Wade, "Loretta Ross"). Ross takes care to emphasize that term is thus inherently political rather than biological. Following this approach, I refer in this book to women of color and communities of color based on their social and political context.

I argue that queer motherwork, a melding of theories of queer and care politics, can offer a means of articulating a form of identity politics that is overtly about justice, power, and praxis. It can help challenge the violent narcissism of white nationalism and elucidate why the work of groups ranging from Combahee River Collective to Black Lives Matter is fundamentally a search for justice that must be named. The queer critique that political scientist Cathy J. Cohen develops through her essays "Punks, Bulldaggers, and Welfare Queens" and "What Is This Movement Doing to My Politics?" addresses the limits of a narrow identitarian politics pursued by mainstream U.S. lesbians and gays in the

1990s. She posits that "the direction our politics will take, while undoubtedly informed by our identity, must extend beyond our particular circumstances and take root in a larger vision of how we actualize, at the very least, a just and equal society" ("What Is," 115).

While Cohen signals that identity cannot be ignored or dismissed, she also points to the ways it can serve as one part of a broader impetus for pursuing fundamental justice across groups. She calls for a "transformational coalitional politics" based in relationality and mutual aid. Central to Cohen's understanding of queer politics is her belief that it needs to be organized around issues commonly seen as falling outside of sexual and gender identity, whether it be workers' right to organize or the rights of people receiving public assistance ("Punks," 162; "What Is," 1999, 116). Building on these ideas, she established the Black Youth Project 100 in Chicago, which supports youth as they take on a radical Black, queer, and feminist politics that challenges racism in Chicago and the broader United States and builds coalitions with groups such as undocumented youth.

This queer reading of identity as a basis for coalitional work is complemented by sociologist Patricia Hill Collins's theorizing of motherwork. She conceptualizes motherwork as public action that extends beyond families and "recognizes that individual survival, empowerment, and identity require group survival, empowerment, and identity" ("Shifting the Center," 47). Motherwork is not only the efforts by literal mothers to defend their children, work that has been well documented by scholars such as Nancy Naples (*Grassroots Warriors*), Temma Kaplan (*Crazy for Democracy*), and Melissa Wright ("Urban Geography"); it is also the cumulative efforts of a community made up of biological and chosen families, neighbors, friends, and strangers who find themselves taking up a shared cause like improving housing or street safety. This expansive notion of motherwork as extending beyond biological kin resonates with how the members of the Combahee River Collective understand their identity-based politics in their famous statement. While focusing in particular on their own issues, they argue that "the inclusiveness of our politics makes us concerned with any situation that impinges upon the lives of women, Third World, and working people" ("Combahee River Collective Statement," 26). This concern, or care, is a central component of motherwork. Queer motherwork, then, is not about conceptualizing what it means to be queer-identified and a mother. Instead, bridging these identity-based frameworks is a way to contest power and inequity through an embrace of both identity and community. Queer motherwork accounts for activists' embrace of a form of identity politics that focuses on issues of power and inequity, seeking to build coalitions to address injustices across communities, that highlights the dynamics among individual activists, children, families, and communities, and that rejects heteronormativity and vehemently objects to the denigration of mothering and care. Queer motherwork elucidates the practices that activists use—or fail to center—when pursuing identity-based organizing that is grounded in a fundamental search for social justice through coalition and solidarity.

CAAAV activists have long fought for accountability in cases of police violence, including the 1995 shooting death of Chinese youth Yong Xin Huang. He was killed by police while he was playing with a pellet gun outside a friend's home in Brooklyn. CAAAV supported the family as they pushed for the prosecution of his shooter, Officer Steven Mizrahi. They protested after a grand jury acquitted Mizrahi, and in turn, they helped the family successfully reach a federal civil suit settlement with the city. His family became part of a broader effort to address police violence, a key example of the abuse of power and violence against communities of color. Huang's older sister, Qinglan Huang, has practiced queer motherwork since the 1990s, most recently by serving as a leading voice when she joined CAAAV after the Gurley shooting. While some members of the Chinese community saw anti-Asian racism in Liang's prosecution and manslaughter conviction, CAAAV and Qinglan Huang saw echoes of her brother's killing and a critical need for cross-racial solidarity. She said, "Both didn't do anything wrong, and they got shot by police and cut down their lives" (Fuchs, "Decades after"). Huang's approach is an example of queer motherwork; she simultaneously draws on her identity as a sibling, Chinese community member, and anti-police-brutality activist. Her words articulate the importance of going outside the confines of identity-based communities to mark the collective significance of police impunity and the devaluing of people of color's lives by state actors. CAAAV and their allies' early statement on Gurley's slaying also demonstrates a queer motherwork approach in its crossing of the boundaries of community and kin:

> We cannot forget when other communities of color stood with us against the police killing of Yong Xin Huang in 1995 and other incidents of police brutality and countless critical moments our communities were also hurt. We have a responsibility to protect our prosperity by protecting ALL families and that means also the family of Akai Gurley who has lost their loved one forever (quoted in Rankin, "Asian-American Coalition").

Their words, emphasizing a need to support all families along with those of Huang, demonstrate the potential for a queer motherwork that contests everyday forms of violence and pushes for a sense of interdependency and coalitional social justice activism across communities.

In the South Bronx, the country's poorest Congressional district that is majority Black and Puerto Rican, MOM, an ally group of CAAAV, has also pursued queer motherwork. Formed in the 1990s, MOM came together as parents learned about inequalities in funding for their children's education. While never solely a group made up of mothers or fathers, the group used mother-work as their frame. They are a dynamic organization that includes LGBTQ and nonparent or guardian members, and they have built a strong community presence through their work on issues in the schools and in housing. While CAAAV emerged out of the Asian American movement, MOM emerged out of efforts to build community power and support low-income parents of color in New York. Both organizations address issues such as housing inequalities, each formally participating in the Right to the City alliance, and also share a commitment to social justice for their communities. MOM has often collaborated with other South Bronx groups such as Sustainable South Bronx, faith leaders, and alliances that address issues like dangerous trucks driving on residential streets and overpolicing in public schools.

In 1998, MOM members came together in the wake of a tragedy. That year a commercial truck killed six-year-old Crystal Vargas while she was bicycling in her Hunts Point neighborhood in the South Bronx. Her death attracted major English and Spanish media attention, as it showed the danger of the many industrial trucks that rumbled down residential streets in the area (Waldman, "Trash Giant"; Hu, "Where a Little Girl"; Kappstatter, "Moms on the Line"; Martinez, "Crash"). As Vargas' principal Laura Lux said, "Sometimes they [truck drivers] obey the traffic laws. . . . Many times they do not" (Olmeda, "Walk"). MOM and allied community groups pushed the city to respond to this issue by launching a media campaign and by conducting their own research on truck traffic (Portlock, "Asthma"). I discuss their tactics further in chapter 3, particularly their comparison of Department of Transportation commissioner James Kilkenny to the Grinch who stole Christmas due to his resistance to their demands. Using the imagery of a children's storybook villain along with documenting the direct costs of children's safety, MOM activists harnessed the power of coming together, drawing on queer motherwork values to defend the children of their community and demand that their city's officials prioritize safety over industry.

In both of the cases presented, activists participate in a form of queer motherwork that bridges identities and pursues justice for communities of color. I turn to the Combahee River Collective to consider a final piece of queer motherwork practice that offers a sense of what differentiates this approach from the white identity politics that has been used as a base for racist, anti-immigrant, trans- and homophobic, and sexist rhetoric and policy making. "As feminists we do not want to mess over people in the name of politics," the collective members state. "We are committed to a continual examination of our politics as they develop through criticism and self-criticism as an essential aspect of our practice" (27). As Keeanga Yamahtta-Taylor argues in her introduction to *How We Get Free: Black Feminism and the Combahee River Collective*

(2017), building on radical activism and Marxist analysis, the collective sought to pursue an intersectional approach that recognized that "oppression on the basis of identity—whether it was racial, gender, class, or sexual orientation identity—was a source of political radicalization" and that activism was "also about what you could do to confront the oppression you were facing" (8–9). The *Combahee River* statement is credited as being the first to use the phrase "identity politics," and it reveals a complex understanding of how to live and fight in the intersections of identities, oppression, and movement. A reflective, queer motherwork embrace of identity makes it possible for activists to name and address central social justice issues while at the same time allowing them to continually refine the analysis and internal challenges that are at the heart of collaborative work. This book offers lessons from two organizations' histories that demonstrate the potential of coalitional, identity-based organizing and the long-term investments that activists make as they seek to create a more just world.

Pushing Back

Pushed to the edge of the world
there she made her home on the edge
of towns, of neighborhoods, blocks, houses,
Always pushed toward the other side.
Away, she went away
but each place she went
pushed her to the other side, al otro lado.
GLORIA ANZALDÚA, "DEL OTRO LADO"

On a cool, gray May afternoon in 2009, members of MOM and CAAAV gathered with about one hundred other activists connected to the Right to the City alliance, a national group organizing against gentrification and the displacement of low-income people in cities. They came together to announce the release of a report titled "People without Housing and Housing without People: A Count of Vacant Condos in Select NYC Neighborhoods." The rally and a tour that followed brought marchers in front of multiple vacant condominium buildings that confirmed their findings: in the 2000s, areas such as Harlem and El Barrio or East Harlem saw an uptick in both housing prices and the displacement of residents of color, while condominiums sat vacant in tower buildings. As the economic recession of the 2000s left many New Yorkers struggling even more than they had before, it was particularly troubling to see new buildings sitting empty while there were so many New Yorkers who were finding it difficult to stay in their homes. MOM's Cerita Parker rallied the crowd and asked, "Recently, all these luxury stores and condominiums have been built in our community. Who are they for? I can't live in these buildings, and I can't shop in these stores."

IMAGE 1. Parker (left) leading the Right to the City vacant condos rally, May 11, 2010. Photo by Ariella Rotramel.

Parker's words were direct and underscored the challenge marginalized New Yorkers, who were living in a city that had long ignored their communities, faced. Instead of resources being made available that would meet their needs and improve their quality of life, such as affordable grocery stores and dynamic free public parks, expensive retail stores and housing were being developed for newcomers that had yet to materialize, while long-term residents watched as familiar storefronts closed and restaurants and boutiques opened that were priced beyond their means. MOM and CAAAV activists converged on Harlem to protest their communities' needs being treated as a mere afterthought. Their understanding of development schemes was based in their situated knowledge as a heterogeneous group of activists who were willing to contest this reality and voice their hope for a different future (Haraway, "Situated Knowledges," 585). These activists performed a form of queer motherwork, challenging existing power structures and asserting the rights of their community to thrive in New York.

The rally in Harlem was held in the former Frawley Circle, at the intersection of Fifth Avenue and 110th Street, on the border of Harlem and Spanish Harlem (El Barrio), renamed Duke Ellington Circle in 1995 after the famous and prolific jazz artist who found success playing in the neighborhood's clubs in the 1920s. Participants sought to challenge the encroachment of development for high-income residents in the midst of the global economic crisis into areas that had long been economically, politically, and socially erased. These neighborhoods to the north of Central Park were frequently cut off in maps of Manhattan, spaces assumed to be not of interest to affluent residents and tourists seeking to navigate the city. Home of the Harlem Renaissance and more modern Black artistic and political movements, Harlem is an iconic Black neighborhood, but by 2010, it had lost many Black residents, with numbers dropping to the lows of the 1920s as affluent white residents moved in (Roberts, "No Longer"). Similarly, Spanish Harlem/El Barrio's status as a hub for Puerto Rican and other Latinx residents was threatened as developers attempted to rebrand it as "SpaHa" to echo already recognizably gentrified areas like SoHo (south of Houston Street) and Dumbo (down under the Manhattan Bridge overpass). Developers' calling the area "Upper Yorkville" was an attempt to reimagine it as an extension of the Upper East Side (Calmes, "Wary"; Zimmer, "Dividing Line").

The questions Parker asked at the rally as a MOM member spoke to the challenges CAAAV activists were raising in the south end of Manhattan. For these groups, there were clear connections between the vacant condos in Harlem and the larger struggle in the city over housing. Single-resident occupancy buildings have played a significant role in the ability of migrant and/or single low-income residents to live in cities. Mid–twentieth century urban renewal in the South Bronx destroyed these buildings along with low and middle-income housing, resulting in the loss of thousands of housing units; in cities such as San Francisco, struggles over single-resident occupancy buildings like that city's International Hotel in Filipino Manilatown in the 1960s and 1970s illustrated their importance for Asian American communities (Lampe, "Role," 371–72; Liu and Geron, "Changing Neighborhood," 23; Fujino, "Who Studies," 147). New York in the twenty-first century is just another example of this long disenfranchisement of poor communities of color through residential displacement.

In one high-profile case in 2009, New York City officials repeatedly removed residents of the single-resident occupancy building at 81 Bowery. Its residents were removed from their homes because of purported safety concerns, but they were not given information in their languages and found themselves at the mercy of nonprofit services that placed them in temporary housing across the city. As CAAAV housing organizer and later executive director Helena Wong explained at the time, "The issue is that there's no plan and there's no notice.... People are literally yelling, 'Get your stuff and go.' There is no plan to make sure people are in temporary housing, and there's no information on when [they can] move back" (Shapiro, "Displaced Tenants"). While the residents eventually were able to return to their homes, their interactions with city officials made it clear to them that the city was not deeply invested in keeping residents permanently and safely housed. The approach the city took to safety enforcement failed to put residents' needs foremost and instead contributed to an already hostile dynamic they faced with their landlord. CAAAV reported that over a six-month period in 2008, tenants of six more buildings in Chinatown were evicted and sent to shelters. 81 Bowery exemplified a growing disregard for residents' ability to remain in the neighborhood for the long term.

As both MOM and CAAAV activists have sought to articulate a vision and organize for a New York that is livable for their communities, they have rallied under Asian, people-of-color, migrant, and low-income identities and have connected local engagement to global struggles for the rights of those sharing these identities. Their approach has been to build solidarity rather than to homogenize the identities and experiences of their own members and set them against the experiences of others. For example, CAAAV's politics are explicitly pan-Asian, emphasizing shared histories of anti-Asian racism in the United States. At the same time, CAAAV's projects have frequently focused on the particular challenges faced by specific Asian groups such as South Asian taxi drivers and Filipina domestic workers. Moreover, CAAAV has participated in protests supporting South Korean farmers, immigrants, and transgender rights and has combatted police brutality. MOM centered on the needs of largely Black and Puerto Rican residents in the South Bronx, focusing on issues of poverty and neglect by the city. The organization has also frequently prioritized forming coalitions with people of color from across the world to address climate change and with youth seeking to address the school-to-prison pipeline in New York City's public schools. In both cases, these efforts reflect a sensibility commonly found in radical women-of-color-centered politics that seeks to balance the dynamics across collective, multiple, and individual identities and experiences (Moraga and Anzaldúa, *This Bridge*).

This book explores the work of these two groups to understand how and why identity-based organizing led by women of color in New York City built community-based knowledge and action from the 1980s into the 2000s. Identity-based approaches have been critiqued as divisive, isolating, or limited in their ability to produce change (Lilla, *Once and Future Liberal*; Brown, "Wounded Attachments") However, the work of MOM and CAAAV activists suggests the need for a more complicated analysis. Coming together either as people of color in the South Bronx or as Asians from across the city, both groups embrace coalitional work that grows out of the cross-cutting nature of shared struggles. As Maggie Nelson argues, it is common nowadays to discount "anyone who refuses to slip quietly into a 'postracial' future that resembles all too closely the racial past and present—as *identitarian*. . . . Calling the speaker *identitarian* then serves as an efficient excuse not to listen to her" (*The Argonauts*, 54). Attacks on identity politics overlook the institutionalized inequities that continue to harm communities of color, women, LGBTQ people, immigrants, and other groups. Mark Lilla's recent call for an embrace of citizenship does not account for the failure of such attempts or ways they have reproduced inequities within communities, such as in the case of gay marriage. Similarly, Wendy Brown's assumption that an embrace of identity politics is based on "the politicization of *exclusion* from an ostensible universal" does not take account of actors whose identities emerge out of histories of violence and inequity, who need to respond to real threats to their survival, and who envision themselves as part of a much broader "we" whose future might unfold in a polity beyond the liberal state ("Wounded Attachments," 398). Brown offers "wanting to be" rather than claiming "being" in the present as a potential way of destabilizing identity (407). However, members of CAAAV and MOM members want to stay in their homes and neighborhoods and be safely part of New York and the broader world. Thus, their communities' present and future are both at stake. It is necessary to address identity directly when these "wants"—for example, wanting to live without the threat and realities of violence or wanting to breathe healthy air and safely play in neighborhoods—are denied precisely because of the racial, class, gender, and migrant identities of activists (Walters, "In Defense"). Through an attention to these histories and the particular identity-based praxis of CAAAV and MOM activists, it is possible to recognize the potential of an identity politics that is not grounded in the negation of intersectionality or other groups' oppression but rather is an expression of the deeper commitments that are the bedrock of identity-based analyses: racial, class, and gender justice. These justice-oriented values of identifying shared struggles while attending to particular manifestations of oppression are the core of queer motherwork as a form of praxis and offer a means of responding to ongoing identity-based inequities.

Reading across and within Communities

As activists and scholars such as Jo Freeman, Miranda Joseph, and Cathy J. Cohen have shown, group dynamics and community-based work can be deeply fraught. The term "community" itself can take on different valences, as some uses "center around unifying social locations or cultural roots," while "other definitions hinge more on shared interests or common points of resistance" (Haedicke and Nellhaus, introduction, 25). These variations (along with the different lifespans of communities) notwithstanding, a common thread in the meaning and practice of community is that it serves to create an "ethical link" built on these convergences (Haedicke and Nellhaus, introduction, 25). This ethics can be read alongside Benedict Anderson's observations about nations as imagined political communities—that they are "*imagined* because the members of even the smallest nation will never know most of their fellow-members, meet them, or even hear of them, yet in the minds of each lives the image of their communion" (*Imagined Communities*, 3). Centrally, community is about how activists understand their connections to others, the obligation to address social issues, and the importance of building power within their groups and more broadly. "Community" is thus a contested term that continues to be relevant for activists addressing social inequalities. It creates a sense of shared issues and purpose, highlighting that inequity and oppression are not simply individual misfortunes but structurally produced and thus requiring a collective response (Young, "Five Faces"). CAAAV has used both "community" and "communities" to refer to its own work, thus signaling through the latter term its recognition of the multiple Asian populations that make up New York City. For example, former CAAAV organizer and executive director Sung E. Bai referred particularly to Korean and Southeast Asian communities when reflecting on her own journey (interview with author, June 5, 2008). MOM built its sense of community out of its geographic home in the South Bronx. While CAAAV activists have made their homes all over the city, from Jackson Heights in Queens to Manhattan's Upper West Side, MOM's membership is made up of individuals who call the local neighborhoods of Hunts Point and Longwood home. Organizer Nova Strachan uses the singular "community" as the focus of her interest in trying to change her community, the South Bronx, for the better (interview with author, March 5, 2008). For MOM, the work of community that finds solutions for their area comes out of movements for racial and economic justice. This effort has made it possible to bring residents from differing racial, gender, class, and sexual identities together under the banner of MOM. Without a sense of shared struggle, history, and support, groups like MOM and CAAAV would not be able to bring together people to address the inequalities they face over the long term. If we understand that major social issues still affect identity groups in different ways because of how structural inequality works (by targeting and incarcerating people of color and people with disabilities at high rates and by overlooking the medical needs of people of color, low-income people, LGBTQ people, people with disabilities, etc., which leads to their having disproportionately negative health outcomes), then it makes sense that identity-based organizing remains important (Alexander, *New Jim Crow*; CDC, "CDC Health Disparities"). If identity is a foundational component of inequity, then it is necessarily the basis for responding to these outcomes. In order to develop a fuller understanding of how the identity-based work of these groups developed, this study considers the history of each group, identifying the critical issues of their communities and how they have framed them throughout their campaigns. The work of CAAAV and MOM over the past three decades can be further explored by uncovering the forms of advocacy they have undertaken and the efforts they have made to negotiate internal diversity.

CAAAV and MOM are small, women-of-color-led community organizations that have joined a number of progressive coalitions on issues such as housing rights and environmental justice at the local, national, and global levels. During the time that I conducted my ethnography in the 2000s, CAAAV downsized its offices from a former convent in the Fordham section of the Bronx and a shared space in Woodside, Queens, to a storefront in Manhattan's Chinatown on Hester Street, the area it had its roots in. Its paid staff fluctuated in size over that period but typically included an executive director, administrative staff, and at least two community organizers. The membership of CAAAV ranges from highly active individuals to key stakeholders in particular projects to longtime Asian activists, in addition to a broader range of donors. In this regard, the organization resembles Jews for Racial and Economic Justice (JFREJ), with a small, active core and a broader base of supporters that turns out for major events. MOM, on the other hand, stayed in its storefront office on Intervale Avenue until 2018 and then when it moved, it only went a few blocks down the same street. The group has a smaller paid staff than CAAAV; there is an executive director and two to three community organizers, one of whom is often a housing organizer and another of whom is a youth organizer. The membership has largely been made up of residents from the area; the organization has not tended to attract a broader range of members or donors. In this regard, the organizations differ in their primary identity, as CAAAV reaches a broad pan-Asian community that stretches and attracts attention beyond the bounds of New York City, while MOM is neighborhood-focused.

Reflecting the ethnic complexity of New York City's neighborhoods, each organization has a distinct style due to their differing organizational histories and community bases. Taken together, CAAAV's cross-Asian community approach and MOM's grounding in the South Bronx—an area that is predominately Black and Puerto Rican—provide an opportunity to consider social justice history across communities and issues. This emphasis on specificity and cross-cutting histories reflects activists' journeys as individuals and as participants in multiple social justice struggles. Issues like housing inequality are not the problem of one community or racial group. Activists frequently come into contact and build networks that overlap. Unfortunately, scholarship often does not address these dynamics. Excellent case study–based works often center on one racial community or one social issue in a manner that may not sufficiently emphasize connections to a broader landscape (Das Gupta, *Unruly Immigrants*; Sze, *Noxious New York*; Orleck, *Storming*; Taylor, *From #BlackLivesMatter*). This book aims to highlight connections across communities and issues by refusing to settle on one group or topic. Such connections are the norm for organizations that share these values and practices. Efforts to document and analyze how groups productively interact with one another can support a social justice scholarship that is not confined by the boundaries of academic inquiry that continue to limit studies to a particular community or topic. This approach offers a truer picture of the collaboration on the ground between groups like MOM and CAAAV. As research by scholars such as Francesca Polletta and Roberta Gold reveals, just as civil rights activists drew from the work of pacifists and radical unionists and women liberationists learned from leftists and tenant organizers, so too social justice movements have complicated genealogies. Foregrounding these histories reflects the realities of activism and challenges frequently fragmented approaches to social justice research.

Not only is understanding the continued salience of identity-based action critical to this project but so is recognizing the heterogeneity of neighborhoods and ethnic groups with significant internal differences (e.g. gender, class, sexuality, country of origin). These intragroup dynamics and overlaps among communities are frequently ignored in mainstream discussions and histories of immigrant, women, queer, Black, Latinx, and Asian communities; this is evidenced by simplistic accounts of these groups as homogenous voting blocs, interest groups, and populations at odds with one another. Such boundaries have tended to be reified in academia through singular categories, established disciplines as specializations, and the advent of identity-specific interdisciplinary fields. At the same time, other works have addressed Afro-Latinxs, engaged in queer of color critique, and undertaken mixed race studies, thus demonstrating continued efforts to explore these overlaps (Dzidzienyo and Oboler, *Neither Enemies*; Muñoz, *Disidentifications*; Ferguson, *Aberrations*; Puar, *Terrorist Assemblages*).

The diversity within communities also intersects with other groups through shared identities. When communities or community-based organizations are only thought of in terms of one of these categories, these connections are erased and the account of the communities in question fails to represent the complex dynamics on the ground. Importantly, shared experiences of poverty or police violence provide crucial opportunities for making common cause on issues such as tenants' rights. Additionally, collective social justice commitments bring activists together in movements that they may not initially have expected to be part of or interested in joining. Challenging assumed boundaries, MOM and CAAAV activists participated in JFREJ Purim celebrations; they also joined LGBTQ youth of color from Fabulous Independent Educated Radicals for Community Empowerment (FIERCE)—an organization supporting their leadership and power—in a dance in the state capital of Albany, as they took a break from supporting the domestic workers' bill of rights.

Intragroup differences can also produce challenges for community organizing, as tensions may emerge when members are marginalized or there is a lingering distrust based on differing statuses within a particular social identity. There are many stakeholders within communities, and of course, internal conflicts grow out of differing interests, viewpoints, histories, and intersectional experiences. MOM and CAAAV navigated these concerns by focusing on issues brought to them by organizational members, allies, and local residents, as they sought to manage immediate problems as well as to organize building campaigns to address the broader causes. Unsurprisingly, some members and paid staff would flow in and out of these organizations for a range of personal and professional reasons.

Pushing Back is intended as a study of women of color's leadership in organizations that are not singularly identified with feminism. It takes up historian Nancy Hewitt's argument that scholars must "insist on the messy multiplicity of feminist activism across U.S. history and beyond its borders" (introduction, 7). CAAAV and MOM are both part of a broad-based feminist movement; they tackle critical feminist issues such as domestic workers' rights and low-income single mothers' needs for affordable housing. These practices thus clarify that intersectional feminist praxis does not merely pay lip service to multiple frameworks but commits to work that crisscrosses traditional boundaries. This point is clear in the shared trajectory of MOM and CAAAV, both of which expanded from single- to multi-issue organizations in the mid-1990s. CAAAV initially focused on anti-Asian violence, but it evolved to respond to a range of issues faced by low-income Asians in New York City, focusing on youth leadership, housing justice in Chinatown, and the organization of women sex workers and nail technicians. In a similar manner, MOM's efforts to address local school system inequities broadened to attempts to ensure protection for children outside of the classroom, including protests against unsafe streets as well as air pollution that provided the foundation for its environmental justice campaign. Through this identity-based organizing, both groups not only sought to fight the consequences of poverty and racism but to build alliances between seemingly distinct identity communities. These organizations crafted a structural approach to identity politics that was historically new and that aimed to counter the inequities arising out of a state and a national political system that, by the 1980s, rejected War on Poverty programs and did not view racialized or impoverished groups as constituents but rather threats to be managed (López, *Dog Whistle Politics*; Katz, *Undeserving Poor*; Orleck and Hazirjian, *War on Poverty*; Horsford, *Learning*; Alexander, *New Jim Crow*; Sze, *Noxious New York*). MOM's response to environmental racism in the South Bronx, for example, stressed how an area predominantly populated by low-income people of color came to bear high environmental burdens; CAAAV's increasing commitment to getting at the roots of anti-Asian violence led it to become a key site for the organizing of domestic workers' rights. These efforts enabled both groups to see how the legacies of slavery are at the heart of the care industry and to build common cause across ethnic, racial, and national identities. Both groups provide histories of working from and through identities within the shared, transnational context of New York City.

Navigating the Nonprofit Industrial Complex

The bulk of CAAAV and MOM's funding has been from grants and donations. Available Internal Revenue Service 990 tax forms provide a sense of each organization's path as it institutionalized. Once they became registered 501(c)(3) nonprofit organizations, they became tax exempt and thereby eligible to receive tax-deductible contributions. Both groups used the mix of grants and donations they received to support current projects. CAAAV gained its 501(c)(3) status in 1992 and was categorized as a crime prevention not-elsewhere-classified organization because of its roots in fighting anti-Asian violence. Based on 990 tax forms that are publicly available, CAAAV averaged $546,000 in direct public support annually, with a high year in 2008 of over $900,000 and a low in 1997 of $226,877 according to the records available. CAAAV started at an office provided by the Fund for the City of New York with one paid organizer, Milyoung Cho, in the early 1990s (CAAAV, "CAAAV Expansion"). CAAAV consistently has had paid Asian women executive directors: Jane Sung E. Bai from 1997 to 2008, longtime member Haeyoung Yoon serving until 2010, housing organizer Helena Wong from 2010 through 2013, and Cathy Dang from 2014 to 2018. Along with the director, CAAAV typically has had one to two organizers who are paid to work on a project (such as the Chinatown Tenants Union or Southeast Asian Youth Leadership project), and in the mid-2000s, it had an office worker.

MOM became a tax-exempt nonprofit in 1994, categorized as a community coalition under the community improvement and capacity building section. Based on available 990 tax forms, MOM averaged $342,794 from the 1990s into the mid-2000s, with a funding low of $157,863 and high of $517,913. In 1998, the founding codirectors, Barbara Gross and Mili Bonilla, were paid leaders of MOM; there was also an unpaid board. Helen Schaub served as executive director in the early 2000s and was succeeded by James Mumm and Wanda Salaman as codirectors, with Salaman continuing from the mid-2000s as paid director. When its funds were at their highest, MOM also typically staffed a housing organizer, youth organizer, and environmental justice organizer. The funds both MOM and CAAAV raised enabled them to hire a small number of staff members to organize around key community issues.

At CAAAV, there were open concerns about the tensions created by the nonprofit model. As Chhaya Choum, a former CAAAV youth member and staff organizer of the southeast Asian youth project, noted, the 501(c)(3) tax status dictated "what kind of organizing we can do, and what kind of people [can be put] into those roles. I don't think the way the work is set up now allows there to be indigenous leadership. We get paid, and we want people to volunteer. . . . It can be a huge contradiction" (interview with author, February 25, 2008). For poor and low-income Asian members, there are the challenges of limited positions and hiring requirements tied to educational attainment that are normalized as part of nonprofit culture broadly. MOM does hire organizers with a range of educational attainment, but similarly, there is a wide community need for jobs and very limited employment opportunities within the group. As Maria Rivera stated, "This is a nonprofit organization," so if the Federation Employment and Guidance Services, a nonprofit training public assistance recipients, sends "ten people, even sometimes one person, if there's no money to hire that person, well, you got to send them back, and that person's going to go through that same cycle again" (interview with author, July 13, 2010).

In the wake of the Personal Responsibility and Work Opportunity Reconciliation Act of 1996, "workfare" requirements pushed people receiving public assistance into the cycle that Rivera observes. Federation Employment and Guidance Services was established in 1934 to "enhance the employability and the success in the labor market of new immigrants and displaced workers" and became a major site for administering workfare (guidestar.org/profile /13-1624000). But when people are not able to get a position at MOM or elsewhere, then, as Rivera noted, "You have to have the will to go out there and not get discouraged because this job told you 'no' or you didn't have the credentials to get this job and you don't have computer skills, and so you say 'F it.'"

The workfare approach ignores the precarious nature of work, as many low-income New Yorkers struggle to find jobs that can support them (Lambert and Henly, "Double Jeopardy," 70). Groups like MOM and CAAAV serve as a placement option. Federation Employment and Guidance Services workers can help these organizations by supplementing staffing, and the organizations in turn can assist them by providing an environment in which they gain office experience and learn about community issues, a far more compelling option than picking up garbage in city parks. However, neither CAAAV nor MOM is in a position to hire a regular basis. As a result of these dynamics, interpersonal conflicts, and life cycle shifts, people involved with each group either left completely, maintained loose professional connections, or built committed long-term ties.

Coalitions

In the popular imagination, movements for immigrant rights and gender or class equality are wildly divergent enterprises. However, a set of New York City organizations have reliably and publicly supported a range of identity-based causes in recent history. In the 1980s and 1990s, activists drew on their experiences of participating in vibrant struggles against racial apartheid, police brutality, and war —issues that reemerged in the 2000s. Additionally, groups such as CAAAV nourished ties with queer of color organizations that formed in the late twentieth and early twenty-first centuries in the aftermath of the HIV/AIDS crisis. They shared concerns about racial justice and some of their members overlapped. By the mid-2000s, the coalitions that MOM and CAAAV supported constituted a strong bloc of activists that protested such policies as stop and frisk that disproportionately impacted the city's low-income immigrant communities of color. Both groups became part of the Right to the City Alliance whose goal was to counter gentrification. CAAAV supported the work of Peoples' Justice for Community Control, an anti-police-brutality group, and Police Accountability and Grassroots Global Justice, a network of U.S.-based groups addressing working and poor people's movements. MOM youth connected to the Urban Youth Collaborative as they sought to address the school-to-prison pipeline problem. Both CAAAV and MOM supported the efforts of Domestic Workers United and built relationships with other social justice organizations like JFREJ along with the queer of color groups Audre Lorde Project, Sylvia Rivera Law Project, and FIERCE. In the 2000s, they both were part of Social Justice Leadership and had organizers that participated in training programs like Activate! that taught community organizing, leadership, and self-care skills such as meditation.

Organizational Histories

Despite being based in different communities and being recognized for their work on distinct topics, during the early 2000s, these two organizations offered similar structural analyses of the problems affecting their communities and were brought into contact by their engagement in citywide efforts. Though they emerged out of different moments, both groups shared a commitment to justice that would bring them together even more often in the 2000s, as issues such as tenants' rights became increasingly critical. In what follows, I sketch the roots of both groups in order to situate their histories.

CAAAV was formed in 1986 to "give a voice to Asian American concerns about racism, racist violence and police brutality in the New York area and to work with other communities under attack," as its newsletter, the *Voice*, describes its mission statement. CAAAV's mission reflects rising concerns over anti-Asian violence, in particular, the beating death of Chinese American Vincent Chin in Detroit in 1982 (Liu, "Dangerous Upsurge," 4; CAAAV, "Asian Man Murdered"; Shima, "Differential of Appearance"; Kurashige, "Pan-Ethnicity"; Okamoto, "Institutional Panethnicity"; Lien, *Making of Asian America*). Chin was attacked with a bat by two white unemployed autoworkers who presumed he was Japanese and therefore to blame for the loss of their jobs. This assault reflected the anti-Asian attitudes of the period that shifted responsibility for the country's economic downturn away from its political leaders and corporations. Chin was beaten outside the bar where his bachelor party had been held that night and died four days later. On June 23, 2011, the twenty-ninth anniversary of Chin's murder, Asian American Legal Defense and Education Fund's Emil Guillermo reminded readers that the men convicted of the crime, Ronald Ebens and Michael Nitz, "were allowed to plea bargain in a Michigan court to escape mandatory jail time for second degree murder. Ebens pleaded guilty; Nitz pleaded nolo contendere. Both men got this sentence: three years' probation, a $3,000 fine, and $780 in court costs" ("Vincent Chin?"). This minimal punishment demonstrated the unwillingness of the justice system to address anti-Asian violence and would serve to motivate Asian American activism for decades to come.

On the anniversary of Chin's death, I attended CAAAV and other Asian organizations' rally to remember him in Chinatown's Columbus Park. It was a hazy early evening, and about fifty people gathered in the pavilion, while residents in the surrounding park played tabletop games and strolled. The event recalled the violence that galvanized groups like CAAAV and underscored the continued need to address police brutality as part of antihate violence work. CAAAV board members Christine Peng and Scott Lu reflected on this history as a younger generation of activists, and they called for the community not only to respond to individual acts of violence but also to contest xenophobia and other biases that are used to divide working class communities. The event ended with a roll call for the documented cases of people of color in New York who had been murdered in acts of racially motivated violence. One of the names included was Sean Bell. The 2006 shooting death of Bell in Queens by New York Police Department officers as Bell celebrated his bachelor party recalled Chin's killing; both were men of color who were murdered as they were celebrating their upcoming weddings. The acquittal of Bell's killers also resonated with the extreme injustice of Chin's case. CAAAV participated in the significant mobilizations that took place following the Bell murder and acquittal, in keeping with its long-standing work in the areas of antiracist violence and anti–police brutality.

In the mid-1990s, CAAAV broadened its work and developed community-based organizing projects, including the Lease Drivers' Coalition (a coalition of primarily South Asian taxi drivers), the Youth Leadership Project (a program designed to help Vietnamese and Cambodian refugee children and children of refugees living primarily in public housing in the Bronx), the Women Workers Project (a program initially designed to address violence against Asian women sex workers across the city that evolved into one root of Domestic Workers United), and the Chinatown Justice Project and Chinatown Tenants Union (a coalition that mobilized community power for low-income residents in Manhattan's Chinatown).

By the mid-2000s, CAAAV had reimagined its aim as combating "institutional violence that affects immigrant, poor and working-class communities such as worker exploitation, concentrated urban poverty, police brutality, Immigration Naturalization Service detention and deportation, and criminalization of youth and workers" (CAAAV, FIERCE, FUREE, and Urban Justice Center, New York City Anti-Gentrification, 7). The organization thus expanded its relationship with feminist, Asian, and people-of-color-focused movements and began "addressing neoliberal globalization" in its myriad forms (caaav.org /about-us/history-of-caaav). *Neoliberalism* refers to economic practices that encourage deregulation, privatization of state entities, and the withdrawal of state support for social programs (Antrobus, *Global*, Boris and Parreñas, *Intimate Labors*), and *neoliberal globalization* refers to the austerity measures and free trade measures that countries, particularly in the Global South, are encouraged to embrace. CAAAV, alongside other progressive groups, protested these policies, since they further harm impoverished communities, threaten social services, and exploit workers. As the organization continued its work, it began tackling these issues while still maintaining its central commitment to building power and social justice consciousness within New York's low-income Asian communities.

While CAAAV's roots are in addressing violence, MOM was founded in 1992 in response to educational inequalities between schools in the South Bronx and others in the same district (mothersonthemove.org/who.html; Mediratta and Karp, *Parent Power*, 3). It grew out of an adult education program at Bronx Educational Services, during which former community organizer Barbara Gross's adult students were made aware of the poor math and reading scores of their children's schools (Mediratta and Karp, *Parent Power*, 3). With the support of founding directors Gross and community organizer Mili Bonilla, the parents decided to make changes in their children's education and formed the Parent Organizing and Education Project that became MOM. Over the next five years, MOM successfully demanded a school administration overhaul, an equitable distribution of resources, and an end to school board election fraud. In 1996, MOM activists decided to expand its mission beyond educational activism to include "tenant rights, environmental justice, and safe streets" (Rotramel, "'This is like my family,'" 50). Former organizer Lisa Ortega explains that "our issues come from the needs of the people.... If someone complains about the need for a stoplight at the corner, MOM goes out and investigates if this is indeed a community concern. That is how the campaigns come about" (Rotramel, "'This is like my family,'" 50). MOM activists committed to a queer motherwork praxis that would address the needs identified by their community members.

The foundation for MOM activists was their shared identity as South Bronx residents concerned for the well-being of their community, particularly the community's children. MOM activists participate in a form of queer mother-work that includes men, youth, and LGBTQ members while maintaining the centrality of women, and mothers in particular, in the organization, as its name suggests (Rotramel "'This is like family,'" 50–51). In at least one documented case, men's inclusion in MOM caused confusion, as evidenced by excerpts from an interview with a MOM member that appeared in a 2000 *New York Times* article:

> Francisco Perez, 57, a member of Mothers on the Move, a local group that has battled industry in the peninsula, said that breathing can be hard for her, too. "I myself have bronchitis and, at times, it becomes so much worse," she said. "We are waiting for a future when we'll have improvements. It's not easy to work in a community that still needs so many changes." (Forero, "No Longer")

The day after the article was published, the *Times* issued a correction:

> Because of an editing error, an article yesterday about new residential and commercial development in Hunts Point in the Bronx referred incorrectly to a member of Mothers on the Move, a group battling industry in the area. The member, Francisco Perez, is a man.

Members took pride in being a part of MOM regardless of their gender, this rendering the name of the organization a linguistic anomaly. This dynamic both queered motherhood and normalized a respect for women. MOM bridged racial, national, and class differences among its membership through its focus on issues like air pollution and housing foreclosures that are problems for the entire area.

MOM's and CAAAV's histories demonstrate not only how New York's communities overlap both in their membership and interests but also how campaigns focused on a single issue frequently connected to other struggles. These interlocking issues provided an opportunity to collaborate within and across groups. In the 2000s, MOM brought together some of its key organizing concerns through its work around public housing. As noted in a May 6, 2011, post by MOM,

> More than two-thirds of public housing tenants responding to a survey conducted by Mothers on the Move and the Urban Justice Center earlier this year said they want jobs that would help improve housing conditions and air quality. Nearly all identified poor air quality as a factor contributing to health problems in their buildings. ("City Owes")

Through such studies, MOM demonstrated the need for a holistic response to issues in the South Bronx and also made it clear that residents were aware that issues like low employment and poor air quality were connected. MOM's efforts bear out Aida Hurtado's claim that "women of color are more like urban guerillas trained through everyday battle with the state apparatus" as they navigate a complex system that does not have their needs at heart (quoted in Sandoval, *Methodology*, 58). A local waste processing plant had operated without permits for years, emitting a stench that wafted throughout the neighborhood. Over the course of a decade-long campaign to force the closure of the plant, MOM sought to address an issue that troubled residents daily and affected their long-term health. In 2010, the group succeeded, and during the celebration of its victory, MOM member Cerita Parker declared that "although we are local, we also want to be part of a broader picture," adding "whether it's the South Bronx, south side of Chicago, southeast LA, or South America, when it affects people of low economics, it's no longer just a South Bronx story" (Mackenzie, "Sweet Smell").

People living in the South Bronx had been isolated as a community, experiencing oppression as a never-ending and singular experience on the sociopolitical margins of New York. They had been pushed aside and erased as citizens, perpetually rendered as being "alien" in relation to affluent and white New Yorkers. Through groups like MOM and CAAAV, community members have now become activists that are pushing back, demanding resources and respect and finding common cause with people that not only share struggles but strategies across the globe.

Developing an Intersectional and Interdisciplinary Approach

The five boroughs of New York City offer a particularly rich site for intersectional social justice activism because of their demographic heterogeneity and because the city has a relatively accessible public transportation system. I first encountered CAAAV while providing protest security support for the first Trans Day of Action organized by the Audre Lorde Project on June 24, 2005. As a member of JFREJ, I had volunteered and received training on how to work as a team with activists from a range of groups to help participants safely cross busy streets and, as necessary, serve as a buffer between the group and the police. CAAAV activists had helped lead the training and were a powerful presence on the day of the protest, identifiable by their orange vests with "Justice" emblazoned on the back. Hyun Lee, a CAAAV member, highlights the group's coalitional rationale: "The U.S. is building military bases around the world, they are confiscating land from indigenous people and forcing young girls into sweatshops. We so desperately need each other, so that together we can work for the righteous cause of justice" (Dowell, "First Trans Day"). When I began thinking through my dissertation project, I realized that CAAAV would make an excellent case study owing to its clear articulation of intersectional politics and willingness to engage across communities in New York.

I was introduced to MOM when I was riding the train from New Brunswick, where I was teaching as a Rutgers graduate student, back to New York, where I lived after completing my coursework. As happened every so often, I ran into Edgar Rivera Colón, a graduate student in anthropology. He was always gregarious and thoughtful in our conversations, despite our differences in age and experience. We chatted about my developing idea for a dissertation project. I explained how I was interested in doing archival work with women-led nonprofit organizations and particularly wanted to think about issues in cross-community and cross-racial ways. Edgar started telling me about his experiences with MOM; he lived in the Bronx and had previously been a board member. He emphasized the group's legacy of a powerful mix of Latinx and Black women's leadership and offered to connect me to the group. I was fortunate that CAAAV and MOM proved to be organizations that were willing to open their doors to me and share their work.

During the 2000s, I had participated in and then studied progressive activism across identity groups in New York City, resulting in this project. My own identities were a mix of privileged and marginalized positionalities that had prompted me to pursue coursework and activism through which I could negotiate these complex dynamics. Primarily, my racial, class, educational, and citizenship privilege necessitated that I take responsibility for my ignorance, presumptions, and bias that were a part of my socialization. In spaces where the work was intersectional, I had to accept that there could be connections between me and others based on shared identities or experiences but that there could also be boundaries or chasms between us resulting from differences, particularly from my privileged statuses. Both in Chicago, where I attended high school and college, and New York, these were difficult challenges, but I recognized that the discomfort I experienced because of where I was in my (un)learning was far less important than the everyday horrors of oppression that were layered into the lives of people of color, undocumented people, and migrants.

As a graduate student, I ran through a series of dissertation topics in which these complexities would figure, attempting to find a project that was intellectually and politically important to me. During a time when the wars in Afghanistan and Iraq continued, immigration reform was going nowhere, and the prison industrial complex and trans rights came under increasing attack, I sought work that would help me make connections so I could participate in efforts to address these injustices. Moreover, I wanted to do work that documented the knowledge coming out of communities and occupy the position of learner rather than expert. As a result, I took up this project because I was aware that nonprofits do not have the time and resources to record their own histories, and there is a need for more work that focuses on the critical knowledge generated by social movements and the organizations that support them. Despite the ongoing gaps in my knowledge and analysis, I hope that this project serves to highlight the valuable social justice activism that groups like MOM and CAAAV engage in every day to heal our world.

Telling MOM's and CAAAV's stories demands a wide range of sources. I gathered and organized an archive of materials for each group at their offices. I was able to gain a sense of the trajectory of each organization by examining meeting minutes and by researching and organizing materials. I submitted a research protocol and received approval from the Rutgers University Institutional Review Board for the Protection of Human Subjects. I conducted in-depth oral histories with a small sample of six CAAAV core members and five MOM core members with whom I interacted frequently during my ethnographic study. Additionally, I led a group interview with six Filipina domestic workers who were members of CAAAV's Women's Worker Project. These interviews are quoted verbatim and reflect the different styles of speech used by activists, the majority of whom speak more than one language and whose formal educational attainment is mixed. I have refrained from editing their words in interviews and other source materials, as it would reinforce a troubling assumption that consistently using standard English is a prerequisite to being an activist; such editing would also mask the insights and capacities of each person. Moreover, many of the people involved with CAAAV and MOM are multilingual as a result of their migration experiences or heritage. As seen in figure 1, linguistic diversity is a key component of New York City.

I conducted extensive ethnographic research with both groups from 2007 to 2011. I attended political events such as protests and rallies, I undertook advocacy work, I attended organizational meetings, and I participated in community outreach activities such as canvassing, door knocking, and leafleting. These opportunities helped me get a sense of how each group approached their work; I was also able to establish rapport with the interview subjects who were knowledgeable about the topics that my research centered on. I incorporate moments from my participant observation to highlight the dynamics among and approaches taken by MOM and CAAAV activists as they sought to engage residents and respond to the inequalities that were rampant in their communities. Throughout my doctoral work and in the first stages of writing this book, I also collected and reviewed relevant government documents (such as local, state, and national health reports, census data, planning reports, tax forms), nonprofit reports, and media sources (including *New York Times, Village Voice, Daily News, El Diario/La Prensa, Hunts Point Express*) to contextualize the histories of the two organizations, their communities, and the issues they addressed.

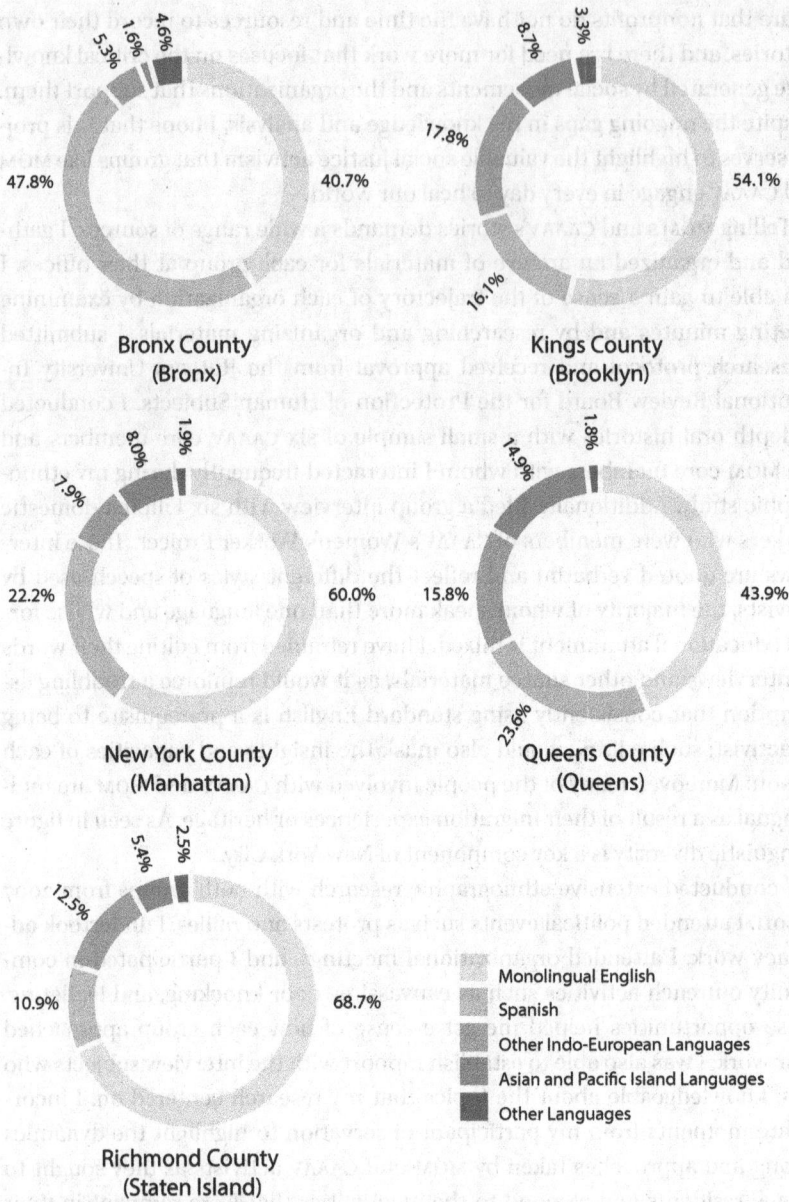

Bronx County
(Bronx)

47.8% 40.7%
5.3% 1.6% 4.6%
17.8%

Kings County
(Brooklyn)

54.1%
3.3% 8.7%
16.1%

New York County
(Manhattan)

22.2% 60.0% 15.8%
7.9% 8.0% 1.9%

Queens County
(Queens)

43.9%
1.8% 14.9%
23.6%

Richmond County
(Staten Island)

10.9% 68.7%
12.5% 5.4% 2.5%

- Monolingual English
- Spanish
- Other Indo-European Languages
- Asian and Pacific Island Languages
- Other Languages

FIGURE 1. New York City estimated use of languages, 2013–17.
U.S. Census Bureau, American Community Survey.

Inequality in the City

Many of the patterns of racial, class, and gender inequality that are endemic in the urban United States naturally manifest themselves in New York, one of the country's largest cities. New Yorkers earning up to $69,000 a year competed with low-income residents in affordable housing lotteries, and the poorest communities, such as the South Bronx, bear overwhelming environmental burdens and staggering unemployment rates, as they support the city's economic strength. Between the 1980s and 2010s, New York's political leadership sought to attract and support upwardly mobile citizens and to encourage global tourism as ways of revitalizing the city. The city's overall poverty rate was stable during this period—20% in 1980 and 21.2% in 2014 (Eide, *Poverty*, 1). New York City has created its own poverty measure to address the high cost of living, and its "poverty threshold for a 2-adult, 2-child family in 2015 was $31,756" (NYC Opportunity, *New York City Government Poverty Measure*, 3). The Mayor's Office for Economic Opportunity's measure found that the number of New Yorkers living in or near poverty was 44.2% in 2015 (NYC Opportunity, *New York City Government Poverty Measure*, 4). Between 2010 and 2015, there was an increase in poverty among naturalized citizens and Bronx residents (NYC Opportunity, *New York City Government Poverty Measure*, 4). Differences were apparent across races in the 2015 New York City poverty rates with non-Hispanic Blacks at 21.2%, non-Hispanic Asians at 23.4% (a significant drop from 2014's 26.6%), and Hispanics of any race at 24.6%, in contrast with a non-Hispanic whites rate at 13.3% (NYC Opportunity, *New York City Government Poverty Measure*, 15).

The measures by borough demonstrate that while Bronx poverty increased, there were significant drops in all other boroughs. The rates of New York City–defined poverty in 2015 were 27.5% for the Bronx, 21.2% for Brooklyn, 18.4% for Queens, 15.6% for Staten Island, and 14.4% for Manhattan (NYC Opportunity, *New York City Government Poverty Measure*, 16). These statistics suggest both race and borough were important factors in New Yorkers' levels of poverty.

During the 1990s and 2000s, the income gap grew across the United States; the poor and middle class saw slowing in income growth, while the super-rich, typically defined as the top 1% in income, saw sharp rises in income (Leonhardt, "Our Broken Economy"; Volscho and Kelly, "Rise of the Super-Rich"). Moreover, communities of color continued to be disproportionately impoverished across the United States (kff.org/other/state-indicator/poverty-rate-by-raceethnicity). By 2008, the top 3% of households with an income of $200,000 or more were particularly concentrated in New York City and the broader metropolitan area, with zip codes in Manhattan being home to the most wealthy (Wial, "Where the 1% Live"). Between 2010 and 2017, it was reported that rents increased twice as fast as wages; that low-priced rental units rose the most

Non-Hispanic White
13.3%

Non-Hispanic Black
21.2%

Non-Hispanic Asian
23.4%

Hispanic Any Race
24.6%

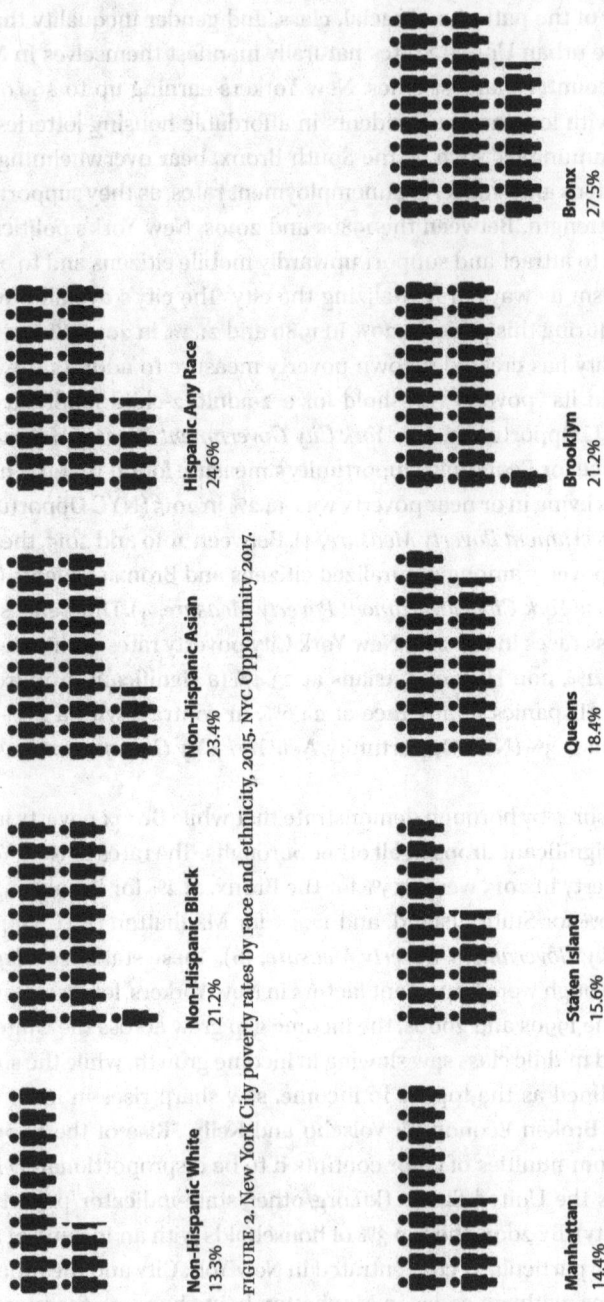

FIGURE 2. New York City poverty rates by race and ethnicity, 2015. NYC Opportunity 2017.

Manhattan
14.4%

Staten Island
15.6%

Queens
18.4%

Brooklyn
21.2%

Bronx
27.5%

FIGURE 3. New York City poverty rates by borough, 2015. NYC Opportunity 2017.

rapidly in cost (4.9% versus 3% for highest-priced units), and that people at the bottom 20% of wage earners saw the lowest increase in wages while top earners saw the highest increases (StreetEasy, "Rents"). Communities viewed largely as a source of cheap labor or as home to members of a stubborn under-class fell outside of the economic development vision of New York's political and financial leaders for the city's twenty-first-century resurgence. This po-litical mapping of New York was underscored by efforts to rebrand the South Bronx as "SoBro."

Simultaneously, Manhattan's Chinatown was subsumed into "the LES" (Lower East Side), an area that had been home to waves of Jewish and Puerto Rican immigrants in the twentieth century but subsequently became associ-ated with the arts and, in turn, gentrification (Cohen-Cruz, *Remapping Per-formance*, 133). These communities were rebranded to attract developers and upper-class residents to the neighborhoods. The marginalization of these communities demanded the connections that groups such as MOM and CAAAV made in their activism. The specific histories of MOM and CAAAV as New York grassroots organizations that I provide underscore the way the issues I focus on are intertwined in the lives of everyday New Yorkers as well as how the movements MOM and CAAAV are part of similar movements in communities across the United States and the world.

In the latter part of the twentieth century and into the new millennium, New York City, along with other U.S. and global cities, fought to secure its fu-ture during a period of massive change in its economic drivers. In the 1800s, New York's population, connections to Europe, strength as a port, and agglom-eration of business activities enabled it to outpace Philadelphia as the U.S.'s global city (Glaeser, "Urban Colossus"). Throughout most of the twentieth cen-tury, it remained a center of U.S. global business and culture. However, during the 1960s and 1970s, the city, like its counterparts across the country, faced major economic and social challenges that seemed to threaten its future. Man-ufacturing declined, including in fields such as the garment industry that had been a key component of New York's economy. While blue-collar industries died out, New York continued to be home to key U.S. corporations and their employees (David, *Modern New York*, 11). During his tenure (1966–73), Mayor John Lindsay embraced both a business tax and income tax to shore up the city's budget. These moves had the unintended consequence of further injur-ing manufacturing while making the securities industry a vital source of funds (David, *Modern New York*, 17). At the same time, the city's service industry and business services industry grew despite some financial institutions being established outside of the city itself (Glaeser, "Urban Colossus," 22; Cannato, *Ungovernable City*, 552). Thus, New York built on its strengths in business to market itself as a city "oriented around finance and corporate management" (Glaeser "Urban Colossus," 20). The outsized role of business in the city's life was also reflected in the significant foreign investment in New York real estate that began in the 1980s and has not let up, even during moments of economic disruption (Zukin, *Naked City*, 23). Business industries became key drivers of employment for wealthy New Yorkers in Manhattan, while the populations in the outer boroughs shifted further into service-related jobs including health and education, these two areas becoming the largest sector of employment in the 2000s (David, *Modern New York*, 6).

The spread of super-rich New Yorkers in the 1990s and early 2000s produced a form of hypergentrification in areas that already were upper middle class, increasing the chasm between affluent New Yorkers and New Yorkers who struggled to pay their bills, over half of their income being swallowed up by rent, and to defend themselves against antagonistic landlords and companies (Zukin, *Naked City*, 9; DiNapoli, "*Housing Affordability*"). In *Naked City* sociologist Sharon Zukin observes that as New York attempted to become a hybrid city with a dynamic mix of residents, it did not "do enough to protect the rights of residents, workers, and shops—the small scale, the poor, and the middle class—to remain in place. It is this social diversity, and not just the diversity of buildings and uses, that gives the city its soul" (31). These tensions occurred alongside the doubling of the foreign-born population of New York between 1970 and 2008 to three million people in tandem with a decrease in the native-born population by over a million (DiNapoli and Bleiwas, *Role of Immigrants*). Census data for 2013–17 estimates that during that period 35.3% of residents in Bronx County, 36.9% of residents of Brooklyn, 47.5% of residents of Queens County, 28.9% of New York County–Manhattan residents, and 22.2% of residents of Richmond County–Staten Island were foreign born (factfinder .census.gov/faces/tableservices/jsf/pages/productview.xhtml?src=bkmk). Immigrants are well represented both in the corporate class of New York and in the health and service industries that meet residents' needs. This revival of immigration is particularly noteworthy, as immigration restrictions and the decline of manufacturing had curtailed the numbers of immigrants into New York between 1920 and 1970 (Glaeser, "Urban Colossus," 19). This recent period is marked by both a shift in the economic foundations of the city to the business sector, a shift that threatens the long-term health of the city and its residents, and increasing migration, so that the place of people who are poor and/or working-class, new or old immigrants, and/or people of color has become a question mark.

The challenges facing poor and working-class immigrants and people of color in New York that have been exacerbated by the changing economic landscape make achieving racial justice more urgent than ever. Anthropologist Julian Brash notes that while, during the twentieth century, New York had committed itself to ensuring quality of life for working-class whites, people of color's demands for the same resources in the late 1960s foundered due to a mix of racism and economic crisis (*Bloomberg's New York*, 27). Countering the tendency in popular and academic works to treat these communities as secondary to a core story of New York City, I place them at the heart of my study, attending to the particular ways that racialized native-born and migrant communities experienced and responded to the shifting tides of economic, social, and political life in New York City. Latinx, Black, and Asian New Yorkers' experiences provide an opportunity to take a cross-identitarian and intersectional approach to 1980s and 1990s activism. This book rereads New York City's recent history in order to explicate the context within which MOM and CAAAV emerged and grew. This period was marked by continuing marginalization, new challenges, and opportunities for successful social justice organizing. While other issues that garnered sustained mainstream attention, such as criminal justice and education, are important throughout this period, the triad of housing, work, and environmental inequality threatened the very ability of immigrants of color to inhabit this city as it underwent redevelopment. These topics are key battlegrounds, as activists seek to counter neoliberal efforts to turn New York City into a 24/7 profit-making center. This acceleration of late capitalism has largely failed to improve the status of the New Yorkers that are at the core of this study; it has also prompted these groups to protect the spaces that their communities occupy and to continue to demand changes they hope will create a future New York City where their communities not only survive but thrive. These aims are based in a refusal to accept that their status vis-à-vis race, gender, class, and nation renders them less worthy or significant as New Yorkers.

Organizations like CAAAV and MOM are just two of a number of groups demanding accountability from the city's leadership. While Democrats dominated the local political landscape and faced little competition from contenders for such elected positions as borough president, over this period there was significant competition in Democratic mayoral primaries (Brecher et al., *Power Failure*, 74–75). Moreover, the repeated election of Rudolph Giuliani (Republican) and Michael Bloomberg (whose career took him from Democrat to Republican to independent as he pursued the mayorship) as mayor indicates the willingness of New York voters, in contrast to voters in counterpart cities like Chicago and Los Angeles, to elect mayors across party lines. Due to these dynamics, New York City mayors have both played a central role in framing issues and promoting policies important to low-income communities of color, and they have found themselves a key target of community activism. Mayors' support for improving the lives of the poor and the working class, immigrants, and communities of color ebbed and flowed in Post–World War II New York.

New York mayors have long attempted to manage a class- and racially polarized city without addressing the root causes of inequality. Their leadership approach has been fragmented, at once attempting to ameliorate some of the most troubling conditions faced by impoverished communities while simultaneously seeking to make such communities invisible in their attempts to attract a wealthier electorate and tax base. For example, Mayor Abraham Beame's administration used "planned shrinkage" to cut social services on the margins of New York City in response to the city's budget crisis in the mid-1970s (Carroll, *Mobilizing*, 14). The 1980s embrace of conservatism at the local, state, and national levels heralded deeper cuts in governmental resources and a further turn to foundations and the formal nonprofit sector. Ed Koch famously stated, "We're not catering to the poor" (Carroll, *Mobilizing*, 17). This hostility is apparent in such conflicts as that of the Lower East Side's Tompkins Square Park, which served as an encampment for many homeless people until Mayor David Dinkins evicted them on the morning of June 3, 1991. As activists chanted, "Housing is a human right," Dinkins had the park secured via chains and police, then defended his action by "alleging that Tompkins Square had been stolen from the community by the homeless" (Smith, "New City," 63; Moynihan, "Turning Point"). Mayor Rudolph Giuliani used his Quality of Life campaign to have police kick out Manhattan Chinatown fruit and vegetable vendors from the triangle at Canal, Baxter, and Walker streets, and the space was turned into an "Explore Chinatown" kiosk by Mayor Michael Bloomberg's administration (Hicks, "Giuliani Broadens Crackdown"; www.renewnyc.com /Newsletters/March2005/).

The efforts to "clean up" New York and make it more palatable for tourists and investors put more strain on low-income residents. A 2013 WNYC public radio series titled "New York Remade: The Bloomberg Years" reported on the downward trajectory of affordable housing in New York City during Bloomberg's administration that began in 2002. Approximately 46% of New Yorkers were "near poor" in 2020, and by 2011 nearly a third of residents were "severely rent burdened," meaning that more than half of their monthly income went to paying rent (see figure 4). The 2013 American Housing Survey estimated that New York City median monthly housing costs as a percent of household income were between 27% and 30%, and monthly housing costs were $1,335.

Informal Bloomberg advisor Professor Mitchell Moss responded to criticism of the city's rising living costs by saying that "1.6 million people live on Manhattan. The rest live elsewhere. And we've made elsewhere more attractive" (Keller, "Bloomberg Legacy"). In other words, low-income residents were welcome to live outside the heart of the city, and migration due to rising costs was acceptable because it meant the wider city's quality of life improved. This narrative provided mayors and their proxies a way of rationalizing an approach to urban development that prioritized affluence over economic diversity and that led to the continued neglect of impoverished areas and rents rising across the city.

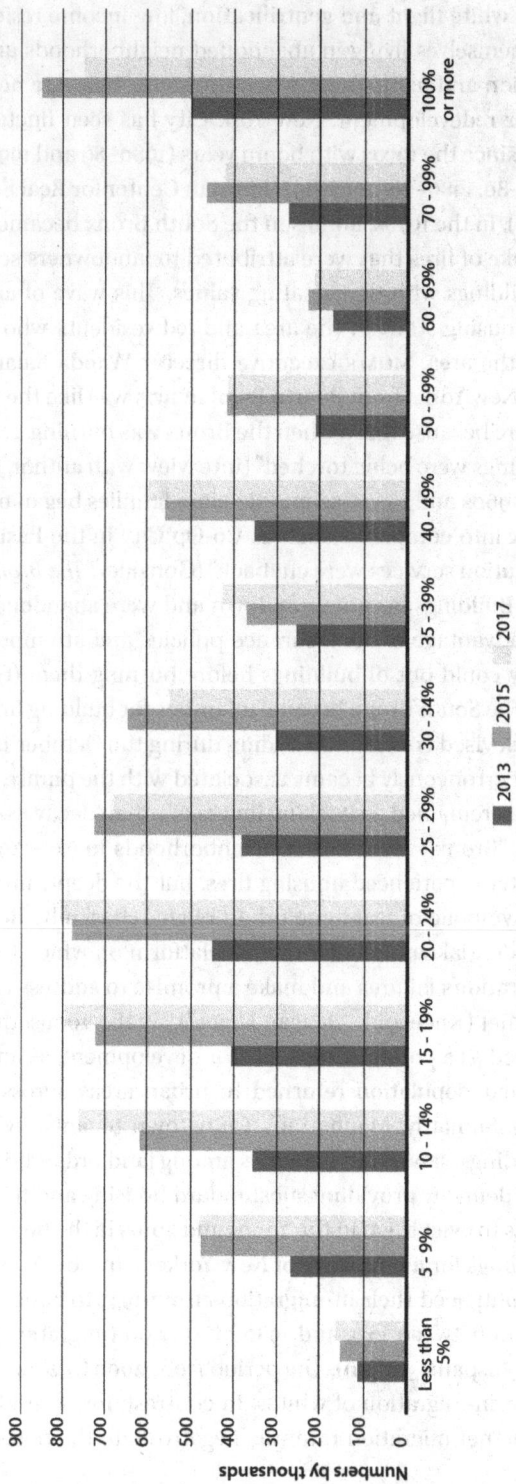

FIGURE 4. Monthly housing costs as a percent of household income, 2013–20. U.S. Census Bureau, American Housing Survey.

As a result of white flight and gentrification, low-income residents in New York City find themselves living in abandoned neighborhoods and subject to economic coercion and harassment when the same areas are newly found to be of interest for redevelopment. New York City has seen fluctuations in its housing market since the 1970s with boom years (1980–89 and 1996–2006) and bust years (1974–80, 1989–96, 2007–13) (Furman Center for Real Estate and Urban Policy, *State*). In the 1970s, homes in the South Bronx became increasingly unsafe in the wake of fires that were attributed to landowners seeking to find a way out of buildings with depreciating values. This wave of arsons shrunk the affordable housing stock in the area and led residents who could afford to leave to flee the area. MOM's executive director Wanda Salaman recalled that "coming to New York [from Puerto Rico] in 1975 was like the worst year to come around here because that's when the Bronx was burning. . . . That's when a lot of the buildings were being torched" (interview with author, July 15, 2008). During the late 1960s and 1970s, as middle-class families began moving out of the South Bronx into complexes such as Co-Op City in the East Bronx, "fire, police, and sanitation services were cut back" (Gonzalez, *The Bronx*, 121; Wynn, "South Bronx"). Buildings became run down and were abandoned, and some landlords took advantage of lax insurance policies and attempted to extract as much as they could out of buildings before burning them (Gonzalez, *The Bronx*, 125–26). The South Bronx became infamous for building fires during the 1970s through televised coverage, including during the October 12, 1977 World Series game that erroneously became associated with the phrase "the Bronx is burning"; this has remained a shocking image of urban decay associated with the area (Flood, "Bronx," 2010). Other neighborhoods in New York and cities across the country experienced housing fires, but the deeply impacted South Bronx became symbolic of fearsome urban blight, chosen by Ronald Reagan in his 1980 presidential campaign tour as a platform on which to criticize the Carter administration's failures and make a promise to address urban poverty that was never met (Kneeland, "Reagan Urges"). By the 2000s, this same area came to be viewed as a potential next site for development, as an increasingly white and affluent population returned to urban areas across the country (Westcott, 2014). Similarly, Manhattan's Chinatown tenants, living in poorly maintained buildings, saw a shift in tactics among landlords who attempted to exploit poor residents by providing substandard housing and then undertook aggressive efforts to evict them in the 2000s and 2010s in the hopes of reconfiguring their buildings for a new wave of New Yorkers. In New York City, whites' out-migrations outpaced their in-migrations from 1935 to 2000, with a major net out-migration between 1975 and 1980 of 324,800 (migration.planning.nyc .gov/#race_and_hispanic_origin). The period from 2000 to 2014 saw a reversal with a net 71,000 in-migration of whites. In contrast, for both Black and Latinx residents, the net migration rate was negative into the post-2000 period.

From 1975 onward, Asians in-migrated due to shifts in immigration policies. Such patterns have dramatically changed the demographics of New York, as the historic Black neighborhood of Harlem became majority white and the Chinatowns of the outer boroughs of Queens and Brooklyn rapidly grew in the wake of the squeeze in Manhattan.

Alongside privately owned housing, the New York City Housing Authority (NYCHA) is the largest public housing authority in the country, serving 583,358 New Yorkers in public housing and section 8 programs and providing 6.8% of the city's rental housing as of 2017 (NYCHA, *NYCHA 2018 Fact Sheet*). New York public housing over the course of its eighty-year history reflects the larger national picture, as it increasingly became racially and economically segregated, neglected, and demonized in the popular imagination. During the early period of public housing, unions built affordable housing for their members (e.g., the East River Houses on the Lower East Side), isolating white ethnic workers from others, and public housing developments were frequently racially and class homogenous (Carroll, *Mobilizing*, 27). By the 1970s, cases of outright neglect and abandonment by private owners and public housing authorities put both the health and safety of residents at risk. By the 2000s, public housing residents' long-standing concerns about inadequate maintenance of their buildings became coupled with fears stemming from contemporary privatization efforts in other cities like Chicago. Hurricane Katrina in New Orleans displaced many public housing residents, and they have encountered significant challenges to returning home (Fessler, "After Katrina"; McClain, "Former Residents"). As part of the Right to the City Alliance, MOM and CAAAV activists memorialized the catastrophe and noted the potential for a similar crisis to occur in New York, which proved prescient in the wake of Hurricane Irene in 2011 and Hurricane Sandy in 2012. Under the Bloomberg and De Blasio administrations, the city began leasing public housing land to developers as part of a broader privatization plan. The future of affordable housing was in doubt for residents; rents for private housing continued to rise through the 2000s and 2010s despite the Great Recession, as developers looked to attract high-income renters (Gonen, "NYC Rents"). The dual forces of gentrification and privatization put further strains on the communities that CAAAV and MOM organized. Mayor De Blasio's promise to balance the preservation of affordable housing with a push for development was met with skepticism by many who saw his efforts as insufficient to turn the tide (Goodman, "De Blasio Expands"). Gentrification and displacement are at the heart of a reading of contemporary New York City history from the perspective of working-class immigrant and domestic communities of color.

New York City is a valuable site for studying community organizing as it at once reflects the dynamics seen across U.S. urban communities and occupies a unique position as the United States' most populated city, one that has a long history of activism and community formation on the part of immigrants and people of color. As in many cities, significant racial and class segregation continues to mark New York City, while simultaneously it is seeing a resurgence in high-income residents. Within its boroughs, there are great disparities that are long standing, and yet at the same time there is a long history of cross-racial collaboration. Radical Asian American activist Yuri Kochiyama's friendship with Malcolm X and participation in racial justice struggles is well known, and she was a supporter of CAAAV. She praised the group's "string of women spokespersons and organizers . . . [as they] held the rein because of their diligent, dedicated commitment and their ability to get along with people of various backgrounds, ages, genders, and sexual preferences (preface, viii). Similarly, Puerto Rican Young Lords activist Richie Pérez, who cofounded the anti-police-brutality group Peoples' Justice, was a mentor of CAAAV activists. Meanwhile, the long history of fighting to improve schools and building community gardens in low-income communities is reflected in the work of MOM in the South Bronx. The density of New York makes transportation across boroughs relatively easy, and it also offers a range of public spaces for rallying and is home to a dynamic set of institutions that support the work of activists from Judson Memorial Church to the Service Employees International Union. The ability of activists to easily come together as part of mass movement moments such as antiwar protests, immigrants' rights marches, or anti-police-brutality rallies, along with their participation in activist trainings and allied groups' events, assists in bridging differences and supporting collaboration. Moreover, as home to the United Nations and Wall Street, New York offers unique opportunities for addressing global issues from their local to international manifestations.

Interlocking Movements

The histories of CAAAV and MOM are important because they crisscross with multiple social movements that are significant to New York, the United States, and the globe. The following chapters document these overlaps, from immigrants' rights, poverty struggles, and workers' organization to environmental justice activism. The first chapter, "Stuck on Repeat: Stereotypes and Structural Oppression of Communities of Color," sets a stage for understanding why both groups have had to directly confront stereotypes about their communities and the connected inequalities and how they have gone about doing so. It mixes New York and broader racial-gender histories with CAAAV and MOM examples to argue that an important piece of each group's work is to define their communities for themselves and act on this definition. Chapter 2, "Building Women's Leadership: Interrelationality as Feminist Praxis," examines the ways that women's leadership became a defining characteristic of both of these groups. Through an analysis of the narratives of activist women, from domestic workers to Work Experience Program participants, this chapter emphasizes how interrelationality enabled both groups to bridge differences within their organizations and across communities, thereby empowering women to make change. Interrelationality emphasizes connection and collaboration rather than focuses on the individual characteristics of emergent women leaders. Chapter 3, "Organizing Strategies: From the Streets to the Courts," turns to the organizing strategies of both groups, providing a deeper sense of how they enact identity-based strategies in their campaigns from their combating of environmental racism to their fighting for women workers' rights. "Housing Struggles from Chinatown to the South Bronx," the final chapter, takes up housing justice and examines cases from both organizations. MOM's and CAAAV's work in this area demonstrates the common cause they have found based on shared injustices and the particular forms that housing inequality has taken in their communities. In the conclusion I connect CAAAV's and MOM's embrace of identity politics through queer motherwork praxis to larger debates in contemporary social movements and political life.

MOM and CAAAV are organizations that grew out of New York City's distinctive mix of visionary activism and drastic inequalities. The city's history of activism includes the organization of unions by immigrants in the early twentieth century, Black leaders' embrace of both militant and party politics, the Puerto Rican independence movement and support for Chicago's Young Lords efforts, a powerful trans activism from the 1960s to the present, and a broader LGBTQ movement that has struggled over issues of race, class, and feminism. MOM's and CAAAV's histories demonstrate women's cross-community efforts to address injustice and maintain a determined hope for a better future. New York continues to serve as a critical site for understanding national and global challenges; both groups' work suggests that identity-based organizing grounded in a commitment to coalitional responses to neoliberal economic disenfranchisement and state violence is a useful approach to tackling problems that are themselves defined by identity-based inequalities. Queer motherwork practice uncovers these dimensions of power and inequity while foregrounding the ongoing need to care for and defend communities on the margins of New York.

CHAPTER 1

Stuck on Repeat

Stereotypes and Structural Oppression
of Communities of Color

> Misery is when you heard on the radio that the neighborhood
> you live in is a slum but you always thought it was home.
>
> **LANGSTON HUGHES, "BLACK MISERY"**
>
> I have 100 percent Bronx pride, like it's a country,
> like I am the Bronx.
>
> **CARDI B.**

In 2016, the South Bronx and Manhattan's Chinatown garnered attention in national media when conflicts erupted over how each community was represented to mainstream audiences. In both cases, the residents of each community were initially engaged as disposable props. The South Bronx was seen as gritty but consumable and Manhattan's Chinatown as timelessly foreign. The frames used in both of these cases drew on decades of racialized, gendered, and classed stereotypes of residents in the two communities to define them as without the same claims or future to life in New York as wealthy, white and/or U.S.-born people (Yukich, "Constructing"; Nguyen, Basolo, and Tiwari, "Opposition"). In the first case, the South Bronx appeared as background for a hip, gentrified reimagining of the neighborhood by developers seeking to rebrand the area for affluent newcomers. In the second example, Chinatown's residents surfaced as targets of a Fox News television segment that mocked and dismissed Chinatown residents as illegitimate members of United States democracy. Reading these recent cases alongside the longer histories of these communities and the work of MOM and CAAAV, I argue that it is critical to understand how the politics of representation matter in their activism, since the issues themselves alongside the actors are read through lenses of identity (Hall, *Cultural Representations*).

Attempts to rebrand the South Bronx resulted in sporadic protests in the 2010s. There was public outrage from residents, politicians, and even mainstream media when developer Keith Rubenstein threw a 2015 Bronx is Burning rave-themed Halloween party. Drawing on the neighborhood's history of piano manufacturing in the late 1800s and early 1900s that earned it the title of "piano capital of the United States" (Goodstein, "Piano District Name"), Rubenstein sought to rebrand the area as "the Piano District." This approach was just the latest in a series of efforts to market the cultural legacies of the South Bronx while ignoring the concerns of residents—"SoBro" in the 2000s had attempted to reproduce the successful development of SoHo (south of Houston Street), Dumbo (down under the Manhattan Bridge overpass), and the LES (Lower East Side) (Barr, "SoHo, New York"). MOM activists participated in this protest and others, including one in response to the 2016 Swizz Beatz/ Bacardi art fair, No Commission, that included a party hosted in a property owned by Rubenstein. Reportedly, "only about a third of the participants had significant connections to the borough, and no Latinx artists were included," despite the branding of the event as a way for Swizz Beatz to support the area's artists. Developers like Rubenstein were pricing apartments at rates far out of reach of long-term area residents, and so, as MOM's Wanda Salaman explained, the message of the protesters was "do not use artists to sell our community out" (Rodney, "Activists"). Reporter Seph Rodney observed that "all these women (and it was mostly women at the rally) were determined and principled, and refused to see themselves as powerless in confrontations with developers" (Rodney, "Activists"). Taking the lead, South Bronx women challenged assumptions that residents would silently watch as their area's cultural and artistic history was used to sell housing units rather than improve conditions for all.

Southward down the East River, Chinatown residents found themselves the target of an October 3, 2016, Fox News piece by Jesse Watters as part of *The O'Reilly Factor* that combined anti-Chinese and anti-immigrant sentiments that were part of the national presidential campaign with dated stereotypical media representations of Asians including sound bites from "Kung Fu Fighting" and clips from *The Karate Kid* (Fox News, "Watters' World"). Notably, these cultural artifacts do not have a direct connection to New York's Chinatown but instead are part of a flat, homogenizing view of Asians in the United States. As scholar Renee Tajima-Peña stated to *New York Times* reporters in the wake of resident protests against Fox News and a brief Twitter apology from Watters, the piece represented the ongoing dualistic stereotype of Asian Americans: "We are either perpetual foreigners or we are the favored model minority[.] . . . We are a threat or we are docile" (Stack, "Protest"). Throughout the history of CAAAV, activists have run up against these U.S. anti-Asian stereotypes. As the organization evolved, its core membership came to reflect the range of experiences of Asian New Yorkers, and it began trying to address the multiple, overlapping issues that are underaddressed including labor rights, gentrification, and violence.

To understand these contemporary examples of marginalization and exploitation and the protest of activists from groups like MOM and CAAAV, it is important to understand the histories of these racist, sexist, and classist representations. Flat perceptions of these communities, particularly in the South Bronx and Manhattan's Chinatown, have informed how policy makers and journalists respond to their issues and demands. Such portrayals have limited a broad recognition of the extent to which CAAAV, MOM, and their allies have collaborated. Despite on-the-ground realities that necessitate connection to build effective challenges to power and its negative manifestations across communities, too often these communities are imagined as isolated from one another. This chapter explores the terrain of raced and classed representations of these communities and how both groups have challenged these representations and the stakes that are at play in their protest.

These representations revived imagery that circulated in the 1970s of each community as timeless or unchanging unlike the rest of the United States. Their usage suggests that they are assumed to be recognizable and potentially compelling to intended contemporary audiences of developers, wealthy New Yorkers, and media viewers. During the 1970s, the South Bronx faced disinvestment and escalating social issues related to poverty and racism, and Black and Puerto Rican migrants who had made the area their home addressed these problems. Meanwhile, a less restrictive Asian immigration policy combined with the Vietnam War, popularization of martial arts films through the iconic martial arts expert and actor Bruce Lee, and deindustrialization served to further cement a troubled mainstream relationship to Asians in the United States (Shu, "Reading the Kung Fu Film"). In the decades that followed, MOM and CAAAV sought to contest the stereotypes that marginalized their communities, combining policy actions with challenges to the one-dimensional representations of members of their communities and assumptions that they were not able to recognize, articulate, and represent their own interests. The two troubling examples from 2016 make it clear that CAAAV and MOM must continue to push back and claim for themselves the stories and images of their communities.

At the heart of this chapter's history is the question of whose perspectives matter. Politicians', policymakers', and journalists' perceptions of immigrants and communities of color often are tainted by stereotypes and reinforce negative mainstream attitudes toward them. A dangerous chasm thus exists between dominant perspectives and community members' own understandings of their resources, challenges, and needs. As highlighted in María C. Lugones and Elizabeth V. Spelman's classic text "Have We Got a Theory for You!" harmful representations of women of color are seemingly inescapable: "We can't," they note, "separate lives from the accounts given of them; the articulation of our experience is part of our experience" (574). Importantly, as Patricia Hill

Collins observes, "controlling images are designed to make racism, sexism, poverty, and other forms of social injustice appear to be natural, normal, and inevitable parts of everyday life" (*Black Feminist Thought*, 69). This chapter focuses on efforts to contest the oppressive aims and make use of such representations visible rather than allowing a casual acceptance of them to continue without dissent.

As feminist scholars seek to "read against the grain" in order to recognize and analyze competing narratives, it is incumbent to return to Lugones and Spelman's challenge to their white colleagues (Samuel, "History and Theory"). They call for scholars to build an "understanding [of] the text of our cultures by understanding our lives in our communities. This learning calls for circumspection, for questioning of yourselves and your roles in your own culture" (581). The histories of MOM and CAAAV activists are entangled with the racist, xenophobic, classist, and sexist ways that their communities and resulting challenges have been represented, (mis)understood, and (un)engaged. Reading local histories requires contextualizing these complex identity-based dynamics both within the longer transnational histories of oppression and the words of activists themselves as they have publicly intervened. The histories I provide do not attend to the question of whether community activists are "authentic" or fully "representative" of their communities. Rather, they elucidate how oppression has circumscribed the work of activists and reveal the strategies they use to carry out the work that they understand as beneficial for their communities.

Representing and Erasing New Yorkers

New York City speaks to both the aspirations and fears of inhabitants of the United States. In the United States' cultural imaginary, it is at once symbolic and peripheral to the country's sociopolitical narratives. New York is identified as nontraditional and out of step with the majority of the United States, both too cosmopolitan and too dangerous but nonetheless worthy of a patriotic embrace (as we saw with respect to its police and fire personnel in the aftermath of September 11, 2001) (Carroll, *Mobilizing*, 5). In popular culture, it is often represented as a city of crime and violence (for example, *Rear Window, Taxi Driver, Dog Day Afternoon, Ghost, Fatal Attraction*, the *Law and Order* franchise) and drugs (for example, *The French Connection, The Panic in Needle Park, Fort Apache, The Bronx, New Jack City, Kids*), as well as a city of possibility and fun (for example, *The Cosby Show, Sex in the City, Maid in Manhattan, Ugly Betty, Friends, Will and Grace, Seinfeld*). It has been revered as a site of freedom and economic opportunity while simultaneously considered suspiciously unclean, particularly in regard to people of color, immigrants, Jews, and LGBTQ people.

The history of New York migration features major groups that famously established racial and ethnic enclaves in the 1800s and early 1900s as well as smaller groups whose histories are less well known. In the mid- to late 1800s, Irish migrants arrived, followed by European Jews and Italians in the late 1800s into the 1900s. There was an African presence early in New York City's history, and Blacks increasingly migrated into the city in the 1900s. Similarly, there had long been Puerto Ricans and other Caribbean people in the city, but they increasingly migrated in the post–World War II era in the wake of industrialization programs like Puerto Rico's Operation Bootstrap. Despite restrictions on Asian migration that were key to the emergence of U.S. immigration laws in the 1800s, New York's port culture drew Asian migrants throughout the 1800s and 1900s (Luibhéid, *Entry Denied*; Tchen, *New York*; Bald, *Bengali Harlem*). As Vivek Bald argues, many small groups of people lived "under the radar of the immigration laws." They "found homes and built lives," and their histories "thus tell us a great deal about U.S. neighborhoods and communities of color in the first half of the twentieth century—about their heterogeneity, their openness, and the unacknowledged role they played in U.S. immigration history" (*Bengali Harlem*, 10).

For example, Harlem was largely inhabited by Jewish and Italian immigrants, but in the twentieth century it became home to Blacks, who migrated into west and central Harlem, and to Puerto Ricans, who moved into east Harlem, as well as to South Asian and Latin Americans who married into these communities. A visible Chinese presence, largely men, was established in Manhattan by the turn of the twentieth century. Asian migration to New York increased significantly after the 1965 relaxation of exclusionary immigration laws, and a range of Asian communities have become more strongly established in New York City, such as the Cambodian community that migrated in the 1980s and 1990s in the wake of the genocide (Tang, *Unsettled*, 3). All of these groups were stigmatized and faced nationalist, racist, and/or religious-based discrimination when they arrived as well as challenging housing and work conditions. This diverse mix of residents drove New York's industrial growth and its status as a global city.

New York City's economic, political, and social struggles, particularly in the 1970s and 1980s, and the challenges they presented to those seeking to govern it are frequently associated with phrases such as "racial tension" and "social unrest." While this period undoubtedly faced major infrastructural and economic crises and saw renewed confrontations stemming from social inequality, a critical question about perspective needs to be raised. Whose relationship to New York City is foregrounded in these narratives of disintegration and upheaval? Authors like E. B. White, John Steinbeck, Tom Wolfe, Saul Bellow, and Philip Roth identify New York in their fiction as a city in crisis, ugly and deteriorating (Cannato 2001, xi–xiii), a viewpoint that has helped produce a mainstream image of New York in sync with that representation, despite the fact that they were all elite white men whose frame of reference was just one of many. Saul Bellow's 1969 *Mr. Sammler's Planet* titular character complains, "New York was getting worse than Naples or Salonica. It was like an Asian, an African town" (quoted in Cannato, *Ungovernable City*, xiii). This reference to imagined southern European and then Asian and African cities evokes racist and colonial tropes that present such spaces as populated and, after the end of colonialism, governed by pathologically incapable "others" whose leadership is passively accepted by residents. In his history of Mayor John Lindsay, Vincent Cannato draw on Bellow's imagery to support the claim that "by the early seventies, New Yorkers had been inured to high crime rates, welfare dependency, poor city services, and chronic budget deficits as the price of urban living" (*Ungovernable City*, 553). In other words, gone was the social and economic stratification that shielded elites from the long-standing problems that impoverished residents struggled to navigate. Such mainstream accounts of New York's turbulent ride through the twentieth century fail to consider how everyday New Yorkers who are low income, immigrant, and/or of color experienced life in their neighborhoods in times of financial and social distress and growth. A different history emerges when we turn away from accounts that demonize people who receive public assistance or that reduce certain communities to dens of crime. Instead, a narrative emerges that highlights communal bonds alongside struggles to address the lack of economic opportunities and the consequences of the prison industrial complex.

Two key issues are at play in the ongoing marginalization of such communities in New York's recent history. First, it is assumed that members of them either do not have a point of view when it comes to social issues or if it allowed that they do have a point of view, it is assumed they do not have a means of expressing it. Social theorist Zygmunt Bauman has argued that as inequality increases at an unchecked clip, "superfluous" people are excluded from "the realm of social communication" (*Wasted Lives*, 41). He quotes political sociologist Hauke Brunkhorst's observation that "for those who fall outside the functional system, be it in India, Brazil, or Africa, or even at present in many districts of New York or Paris, all others soon become inaccessible. Their voices will no longer be heard, often they are literally struck dumb" ("Global Society," 233). In claiming that people are struck dumb by marginalization, Brunkhorst draws an unsubstantiated conclusion that such people do not have a critical understanding of their circumstances or the ability or will to address them. While marginalized actors are indeed often ostracized by mainstream media and ignored by policy makers and academics, even with the rise of the internet age, activists across the globe regularly organize and challenge the status quo.

It is the unwillingness of academics, writers, artists, and politicians to seek out or fully engage with the range of analyses coming from community activists themselves that creates such an illusion of silence.

The second key problem is that the repeated claim that we are witnessing a newly dysfunctional New York effects a social amnesia that erases both past and present New York City communities. Social amnesia is defined by historian Russell Jacoby as "a forgetting and repression of the human and social activity that makes and can remake society" (*Social Amnesia*, 4). Feminist political scientist Mary Hawkesworth argues that "social amnesia is produced and accredited by mainstream politicians, journalists, economists and social scientists" within a neoliberal order that embraces a narrative of individual choice and ignores the consequences of growing economic inequality ("Global Containment," 58). Such forgetting is enabled by the marginalization of poor people and people of color that has played out across the globe. Leela Fernandes describes how the beautification drives in the city of Mumbai constitute "boundaries of the 'public'" that are "dependent on the politics of socioeconomic class" and how impoverished residents are "viewed as interchangeable with the 'muck and debris' which must be 'cleaned up'" ("Politics of Forgetting," 2421). This rhetoric effectively erases the agency of such residents in the imagination of the speaker and their audience. Such erasures are part of a high-stakes scenario because, as Fernandes notes,

> state practices and exclusionary definitions of community and citizenship produce visions of urban development that exclude poor and working-class communities . . . [and] are fundamentally shaped by the emergence of a model of consumer-citizenship that seeks to displace the political claims of marginalised social groups to resources such as jobs and housing. (2428)

Fernandes identifies a pattern found across the globe as public officials and developers seek to meet economically mobile consumer-citizens' desires for a city they can consume with ease, hoping to reinvigorate their communities with residents who are sources of income for business and the state. Low-income urban residents contribute to their local economies by spending money on necessities like rent and food, spending that increasingly strains their ability to remain housed. Moreover, they provide the labor that keeps central service industries such as health and hospitality afloat. Despite these contributions, these members of communities are seen as disposable and as a potential threat to development plans if they are deemed unruly or an unattractive feature of urban life.

As the aim of urban development in the late twentieth century and early twenty-first century to maximize profits for the private sector has meant that technocrats like the three-term New York mayor Michael Bloomberg that offer business-based solutions to city issues have taken center stage. Leading urban studies scholar Saskia Sassen has marked out these movements, particularly in her theorization of "economic cleansing" that grew out of her early work on global cities that identified patterns of disinvestment and deregulation ("Global City"; "Economic Cleansing"). People that have been economically cleansed include

> the long-term unemployed who at some point simply cease to be counted, the failed small businesses whose owners give up and often commit suicide, the impoverished neighborhood subeconomies that cannot compete with franchises, the poverty-stricken middle-class citizens who may still be living in their modest neat homes but keep losing ground, the young who have given up on finding employment, and more. All these have been expelled from the statistical and rhetorical space of "the" economy. ("Economic Cleansing," 674)

Groups like MOM and CAAAV thus must simultaneously challenge the hegemonic ideas about their communities and the policies that have failed them.

Historicizing Representations and Practices

The social amnesia and economic cleansing practices that are at play in the histories of New York racial and ethnic communities must be understood within the broader context that CAAAV and MOM are part of and in terms of the roles that women play within these communities in particular. Racist and sexist representations have been used to rationalize the widespread abuse of Asians, Blacks, and Latinxs, and the local experiences of New Yorkers are dynamically related to the longer history of these ideas and practices in anti-Asian representations in the United States that date to the 1800s. Across the Western hemisphere, Asians were "targets of some of the first national immigration laws that excluded migrants on the basis of race, as well as victims of state-sanctioned violence, expulsion, and incarceration" (Lee, "The 'Yellow Peril'"). In particular, Chinese women were targeted as a threat in the West, as they were widely suspected of being prostitutes (Lee, "Immigrants," 89–90). The goal of hypersexualized Orientalist stereotypes and policies aimed at controlling women's migration was to prevent Chinese men and women from reproducing and establishing families in the United States. While Chinese merchants' wives were exempt from this classist policy, the law and its logic was the source of one of the most prevalent sexist stereotypes about Asian women.

During the Korean War and the Vietnam War Asian women were sexually exploited, and U.S. stereotypes of Asian women continued to circulate and be tied to military violence. Moreover, racist representations in mainstream and pornographic media helped cement assumptions that East and Southeast Asian women were sexually available to white men and potentially tied to illegal sex work. As CAAAV developed, it had to negotiate the tension between the range of realities for Asian women in New York and the limited media representations of their community. In broader popular United States culture, Asians have largely been invisible. They have not been well represented in television programming, particularly in domestic family contexts or within community, and when they do appear as characters, the racist tropes of the nerdy model minority, sexually available woman, and sexually undesirable man are repeated (Deo et al., "Missing in Action").

As American studies scholars Erica Rand and Leah Perry both note, opportunities to build a more complex understanding of migration have frequently been missed (Rand, *Ellis Island*; Perry, *Cultural Politics*). In the 1980s, Vietnamese refugee teenager Hue Cao won an essay contest about the Statue of Liberty, and at first, he was unable to accept the award because it would have disqualified his family from receiving public assistance (Perry, *Cultural Politics*, 118). This was a moment when the fact of poor Asian Americans and the exigencies of public assistance could have been acknowledged, but instead a donation was made to the family to protect their status and to frame their receipt of an alternative award as purported evidence of a benevolent United States system. This approach of hiding the tension between an individual success narrative and the necessary supports of public assistance for poor families, as well as the lack of resources for undocumented people, served to keep intact a framing of Asian Americans as exceptionally adaptive to the United States and shored up the model minority myth that has been used to erase the fact of poverty within Asian communities and to deny the existence of structural racism and xenophobia (Osajima, "Asian Americans"; Kim, "Playing"). The model minority myth elides differences within the community and renders oppression homogenous; in addition, it also is used to further demonize Blacks and Latinxs as undeserving and underperforming people of color (Perry, *Cultural Politics*, 118). Moreover, representations of Asian Americans reflect this mix of reframing and erasure, limiting the ability of those in other marginalized communities to recognize the extent to which their experiences of navigating public assistance and housing as well as the criminal justice and immigration systems are the same (Nguyen, "NBC Asian America Presents"). Groups like CAAAV have addressed these gaps by including political education in youth programming to historicize the Asian American experience in organizing community projects; beginning in the 1990s, the group undertook projects beyond the East Asian community, engaging with South Asian taxi drivers, Southeast Asian youth, and Bangladeshi public housing residents. It embraced its role as a radical Asian group that challenged assumptions within the community—as in the case of the NYPD officer Peter Liang discussed in the introduction—and contested racist representations of their community.

Rather than being groups with little in common, Asian women and Black and Puerto Rican women are linked via their sexualization. The United States slave trade relied on anti-Black representations that framed Africans as god-less and animal-like, and the dyad of the hypersexual Jezebel and asexual Mammy was used to legitimize sexualized violence against enslaved Black women and their labor exploitation (Nicholson, "Classification," 275). These dynamics continue to play out in popular representations of Black women; the legacies of slavery and scientific racism are reflected in stereotypes that result in the lack of adequate services for survivors of intimate partner violence (Women of Color Network, *Women of Color Network*, 2). Indigenous and Latinx communities are likewise plagued by stereotypes. During both Spanish and United States colonizations of the West, indigenous and Mexican women were viewed as simultaneously hypersexual and at risk of abuse from kin. Puerto Rican women and men were similarly framed as being animalistic and in need of salvation through colonization. Contemporarily, Puerto Rico's population is popularly conceptualized as a mix largely of African, Spanish, and indigenous roots. Migrants to the continental United States navigate a form of racism and xenophobia that is dissimilar from the inequality that on the island is based on color and class (Rivera, "From Triguenita"; Findlay, "Slipping and Sliding"). Moreover, many Puerto Ricans were forced via Operation Bootstrap to migrate to urban areas of the continental United States like New York to seek out low-income labor. This program did not address the economic failures on the island, and the rhetoric of an uncontrollable population boom rather than failed economic development allowed for the exploitation of Puerto Rican women in abusive birth control trials and the coerced sterilization of one-third of the island's women by the 1970s.

The devaluing of women's bodies, families, and ability to make decisions about their reproductive capacities undergirded this explicit denial of women's basic reproductive rights. This sexual/reproductive demonization of poor Latinx and Afro-Latinx women connects to abuses Black women faced in the United States during this period and to efforts to coerce women receiving public assistance to utilize the most risky and long-term forms of birth control (Silliman et al., *Undivided Rights*). Representations of Black and Puerto Rican women as exhibiting an excessive, nonnormative femininity are used to devalue them vis-à-vis their race, ethnicity, and gender.

In the case of the South Bronx, low-income women have been primarily viewed through the nexus of teen pregnancy, single motherhood, public assistance, drug abuse, and poverty. These circumstances are not, however, unique to the South Bronx: as of 2012, "52.2 million (or 21.3 percent) people in the U.S. participated in major means-tested government assistance programs" and drug abuse was a concern across communities (U.S. Census Bureau, "21.3 Percent"; samhsa.gov/data/sites/default/files/NSDUH-DetTabs-2015/NSDUH-DetTabs -SAMHSA, "Results," 1507). Moreover, distilling a life down to these elements erases the shared humanity of South Bronx residents and instead presents those living in this area as a population to be pitied and potentially eliminated. Dr. Antonio Silva, a well-known proponent of mass sterilization in Puerto Rico, moved to the South Bronx's Lincoln Hospital in the 1970s, prompting the establishment of the Committee to End Sterilization Abuse by women of color who sought to defend themselves (Briggs, *Reproducing Empire*). Mass sterilization drives and the increasing incarceration of people of color throughout the 1970s into the present are just two ways elites have tried to contain the Black and Puerto Rican residents of the South Bronx (Alexander, *New Jim Crow*; Crean, "Malleable Environments"). The following sections explore specific cases of how elites have framed Blacks, Puerto Ricans, and Asians in New York in particular ways in order to further stigmatize and marginalize their communities and the approaches that activists from groups like MOM and CAAAV have taken to push back.

Refusing Racism:
Confronting Anti-Asian Bias within the Left

In 1988, CAAAV activists led a campaign to address a Lambda Legal Defense Fund and Lesbian and Gay Community Services Center *Miss Saigon* performance fund-raiser. The musical's plot centers around Chris, a U.S. soldier in Vietnam, who marries Kim, a Vietnamese sex worker, a relationship that produces a child. Chris leaves the country, marries a U.S. woman; after Chris learns that Kim is still alive and has a child, he tells his new wife about them, and they go to Bangkok where Kim is now working and find her and the child, at which point Kim kills herself so that her child can be raised by U.S. nationals (Shimizu, "Bind of Representation," 249). Lambda and the Lesbian and Gay Community Services Center choice to fund-raise using this "arguably racist and sexist play" had the effect of "galvanizing Asian American lesbian and gay groups, as well as progressive Asian American and queer groups on both coasts to protest the show" (Eng and Hom, introduction, 13). Frustrated by a lack of responsiveness from Lambda and the Lesbian and Gay Community Services Center, CAAAV and its allies staged protests, sought to educate the public, and engaged in acts of civil disobedience. Their experience demonstrated that white LGBTQ activists did not take the concerns of Asian community members and allies seriously; they miscalculated that these community members and allies would silently tolerate a negative representation in the name of activism.

In her account of these events in "The Heat Is on *Miss Saigon* Coalition: Organizing across Race and Sexuality," Japanese American lesbian activist Yoko Yoshikawa recounts working with CAAAV's first paid staff member, Milyoung Cho, a cofounder of Action for Community Empowerment in Central Harlem who was trained at the Center for Third World Organizing (CAAAV "CAAAV

Expansion," 1). Cho was also a member of Asian Lesbians of the East Coast, a point that was often not acknowledged in news coverage of the *Miss Saigon* protests. Her work highlights the overlapping affiliations of CAAAV activists. Cho and Yoshikawa used two donated tickets by allies to stage an act of civil disobedience in the theater. They interrupted the performance of Jonathan Pryce, a white actor performing as a Vietnamese pimp, shouting "This play is racist and sexist; Lambda is racist and sexist!" ("The Heat," 42). She recalls a "roar that swept over us as we, unscathed and exultant, emerged from the theater[,] . . . a roar of sheer power, concentrated and raw" ("The Heat," 43). In the "Bind of Representation," Celine Shimizu contrasts this momentary pleasure of protest with Yoshikawa's guilt about being "pulled into" the play's compelling spectacle in (250). In this article, Shimizu raises questions about efforts to shut down *Miss Saigon*, noting that there is a need to address the bind of representation within which "Asian American actors and audiences creatively deploy sexuality in order to destabilize hypersexuality" (265). It is worth considering more deeply why this musical was contested within the LGBTQ community as a flashpoint around sexual, gender, and racial identities.

The *Advocate*, *OutWeek*, and other LGBTQ news outlets provided detailed coverage of the conflict, as it raised serious questions about the status of LGBT of color people within the movement: "Are we as lesbians and gays, as individuals and in our organizations," June Chan and her coauthors asked in *OutWeek*, "perpetuating structures of oppression and exploitation? Can ethics and the fight for justice be put aside in the name of money?" (Chan et al., "Pain," 5). Although Shimizu rightly notes that *Miss Saigon* provides one of the few opportunities for Asian actresses to have key roles on Broadway, the casting of Welsh actor Jonathan Pryce in the lead role of the Engineer, a mixed-race character, muddied that argument.

The center's executive director, Richard Burns, downplayed the affair and blamed groups for bringing the issue up too late for the fund-raiser to be canceled. Activists countered this account and said that the organizers had been approached just a few months after the fund-raiser had been scheduled (McDonald, "Gay Asians," 14). While the center backed out of the fund-raiser in response to the controversy, Lambda continued with plans and was denounced by the editors of *OutWeek*, who noted that "the damage to Lambda's reputation, both within the Asian-American community and among progressives in general, will probably outweigh even the considerable loss of funds that a cancellation would cause. Employees of that organization are already reporting difficulties working among communities of color" ("On Missing *Miss Saigon*," 4).

The protest spread, and a wide coalition developed that included ACT UP, Queer Nation, Gay Men of African Descent, Las Buenas Amigas, Latino Gay

Men of New York, Salsa Soul Sisters, and South Asian Lesbians and Gay Men. As a result of their efforts, Audre Lorde ended up refusing to accept an award from the organization (Dean, "Asian Lesbians"). Lorde stated:

> For Lambda to associate itself with a benefit performance of *Miss Saigon*, a play abounding in racist and sexist stereotypes, performed by non-Asian actors, is a sadly divisive error. At best, it demonstrates a gross insensitivity to the real-life situations of our South Asian sisters and brothers, and therefore to the rights of all people of color, to determine our own images as well as our own destinies. (McDonald, "Audre Lorde," 15)

The efforts of CAAAV and allied protesters to promote a community that did not marginalize Asian people foreshadowed CAAAV's work in the new millennium, when it adopted a critical approach to U.S. wars in Asia, collaborated with LGBTQ organizations, and provided support for Asian women workers. Through direct action, activists like Cho and Yoshikawa found power in making public their discontent and speaking out, refusing to accept the careless racism and sexism of mainstream LGBTQ groups and building successful alliances.

Erased through Stigma

Media coverage of the South Bronx in the 1970s, particularly in the wake of "The Bronx is Burning" story, has largely framed the community as one of crushing poverty and hopelessness. While the South Bronx does face challenges with high levels of poverty, air pollution, and illness, this community is also home to many people who have a loving and pride-filled relationship to the South Bronx. The representations of the area as dangerous or burned out erase the connection, culture, and joy the members of the community experience. In 2016, the *New York Times* published series entitled "Murder in the 4–0: An Examination of the Life and Death of Each Person Murdered in 2016 in the 40th Precinct in the South Bronx" (www.nytimes.com/series/bronx-new-york -murder-40th-precinct). While the series was apparently seeking to humanize victims of violence, it had the effect of representing the South Bronx as a space of uncontrolled violence. Moreover, it failed to address the realities of crime in the city. Data from the city for crime in general and murder in particular in 2016 reveals that the rates in the South Bronx were similar to those in other neighborhoods across the city rather than spectacularly higher (maps.nyc .gov/crime). Representations of the South Bronx as an area awash in violence trade on the conflation of poverty, race, and crime that is commonplace in the United States. Residents are assumed to either be victims or perpetrators of violence; this unchallenged assumption is apparent in coverage that represents them as if they had no awareness of the complex problems facing their community or ideas as to how to solve them. They are often imaged as a population to be managed, if not pitied and perhaps saved; what is lacking is a deeper analysis of the roots of the issues that have drawn attention to the community at particular moments over the past forty years.

Throughout MOM's history, its activists have struggled to get politicians to see that community's members are valued constituents and to encourage media actors to see that they are knowledgeable. A 1995 *New York Times* article by Adam Nossiter entitled "Asthma Common and on the Rise in the Crowded South Bronx" epitomizes the long-standing failure of the media to engage the area's residents and approach the community's issues holistically, drawing on the trope of voicelessness. This dehumanizing framework is referenced in the way Nossiter frames the area's alarming asthma rates: "The epidemic is a singularly quiet one. It has not spawned headlines, demonstrations, advocacy groups or loud calls for public action. One explanation: it is an affliction of the poor, those who have less voice, said doctors who treat it in the Bronx." This description highlights a recurring feature of accounts of marginalized communities whereby experts are seen to "give voice to the voiceless," thus reinscribing existing power dynamics rather than recognizing the knowledge and power of communities. Residents are quoted throughout the piece but primarily to illustrate the issue; they describe their suffering and steps they take to head off attacks. For example, the article reports that Lincoln Hospital's "special asthma room, where patients sit along a wall sucking on hand-held bronchial dilators, is a 'madhouse.'" Residents are described vividly in a manner that suggests they are managed like schoolchildren, representing them as infantile with the image of them sucking on a dilator, as a baby might suck on a bottle. The description of the hospital by an area patient as a "madhouse" evokes ableist institutionalization policies. In this piece, area residents are victims of a public health crisis but are patronizingly infantilized, not treated as people with dignity navigating a crumbling health system.

Despite referring to doctors' concerns about a local medical waste incinerator, the piece dismissed industrial causes of asthma "as a matter of folk wisdom," while highlighting issues more readily associated with urban poverty ranging from indoor air pollutants to family stress to cocaine usage. MOM and allied activists developed a campaign to challenge the government's and the media's dismissal of the role of industrial environmental factors in the area's high asthma rates. By the 2000s, there was increasing scientific evidence that the combination of industrial pollution, including that from waste processing plants and truck traffic, indeed contributed to poor air quality and in turn asthma (*ATSDR, ATSDR Case Studies*). Nossiter's investigative story succeeded in simultaneously highlighting an important health problem while arbitrarily writing asthma off as a symptom of poverty. Instead of simply blaming individuals for being poor, Nossiter could have asked how issues related to urban development, such as polluting industries that were not enriching residents' lives, were threatening their health.

Smearing Residents to Raise Rents

The stigma that South Bronx residents face from the toxic mix of racism and classism is linked to the experiences of Chinese immigrant residents in Manhattan's Chinatown. Chinatown is subject not only to the kinds of racist representations Jesse Watters' piece offers but also to ongoing efforts to push out long-term residents. As part of its attempt to turn over two tenement buildings at 55 and 61 Delancey Street, Madison Capital, a private equity firm, embarked on a harassment campaign against residents, according to CAAAV activists. In 2009, under the Tenant Protection Act, residents filed two group harassment lawsuits against the company. This move was supported by city council members Rosie Mendez and Dan Garodnick, state senator Daniel Squadron, and the work of attorneys from the Urban Justice Center. Residents accused the company of carrying out a pattern of harassment intended to remove them from their homes; according to the suit, the company "called the police to disrupt three tenant meetings; rejected rent and frivolously pursued legal eviction proceedings; and ordered tenants to remove Chinese cultural symbols and decorations from public view" (Lee, "Immigrants"). Esther Wang, former CAAAV housing organizer, describes one such incident:

> At one of the first organizing meetings we held, crowded on the second floor landing of one of the buildings, we were suddenly interrupted by a police officer, responding to a 911 call from the superintendent who claimed we were causing a disturbance. The lawyer who was there with us argued that we were merely exercising our First Amendment rights, that we were breaking no laws by meeting. I tried to placate the officer, a young Asian man, promising we would be quiet. After that, he left, and we continued our meeting; this would happen two more times in the following months. ("Pleasures of Protest")

The suits were successful; they were settled in 2010 and have helped in the intervening years to rein in overt abuses against tenants.

However, for one building resident, Ding Juan Zhang, the struggle to keep her housing was more complicated. In an interview with Zhang in a *Village Voice* piece about her building's battle, reporter Elizabeth Dwoskin notes that "the Chinese and Latino tenants are full of misconceptions about their new neighbors," adding "maybe it's the language barrier, maybe it's not," and she quotes Zhang as saying of "the young and the hip" that "they are nice, but they pay way too much rent!" ("Hipsters"). Dwoskin's framing of the residents as misunderstanding the dynamics, possibly because of an assumed deficit in their English language abilities, seems nonsensical. New tenants' willingness to pay higher rents is a well-established fact, but instead of acknowledging that, Dwoskin describes Zhang as a "retiree," the reference to her age, employment status, and ethnic background casting doubts on her knowledge.

Unfortunately, Zhang's struggles did not result from just her being a low-income Chinese immigrant that dared to organize and express her cultural identity. On top of that, she was accused of being a sex worker in the papers filed by Madison Capital (Wang, "Pleasures of Protest"; Powell, "Her Chinatown"). A mother of two, she was fighting to keep her apartment after the passing of her brother, Jian Gou Lin (Powell, "Her Chinatown," 8) The unsubstantiated accusation that she was a sex worker traded on stereotypes about Chinatowns and Chinese women that date back to the 1800s. According to geographer Wei Li, although "Chinatowns had stimulated social cohesion and ethnic immigrant solidarity," to mainstream whites, they "symbolized racialized minority ghettos inhabited by marginalized, unassimilable foreigners" ("Beyond Chinatown," 31). Chinese women were targeted, in particular, through the United States' first immigration law, the Page Act of 1875. In conjunction with the Chinese Exclusion Act of 1882, these laws singled out for exclusion women perceived to be "Asian prostitutes," which gave rise to a sexist and racist trope about Asian women in the United States that would persist for more a century (Lowe, *Immigrant Acts*; Luibhéid, *Entry Denied*). While for residents like Zhang, Chinatown was home, from an anti-Asian white perspective, Chinatowns were home to vice, including sex work. Similarly, as historian Hiroyuki Matsubara notes, anxieties about Chinese women and sex work, at least in part, stemmed from fear over maintaining racial and class order ("Stratified Whiteness," 47). In Zhang's case, these representations and her status as a single woman fighting to keep her apartment made it easy to accuse her of illegal activity. In a contemporary turn on the histories of Chinatown, her presence threatened developers' plans to institute a new racial and class order by bringing in the affluent "young and hip" residents that Dwoskin mentions in her coverage of the Delancey buildings. Unfortunately, as Esther Wang laments, these efforts have been increasingly successful. Zhang and other residents were no longer in the building when Wang revisited in 2016. Zhang had been successfully evicted after a court determined that she had not proven that she had "'resided with' the tenant in the subject apartment during the two-year period immediately preceding the tenant's permanent vacatur [final vacating of the apartment]," as her brother had moved to Maryland, while she stayed (*BCD Delancey LLC v. Jian Gou Lin*). Zhang's case demonstrates the particular challenges residents face as they attempt to fight the forces of gentrification in contemporary New York. While she experienced a personal loss, she was able to counter the assumption that she would passively accept that her neighborhood was no longer hers by engaging with the media, participating in organizing, and taking her case to court. As the next chapter demonstrates, both CAAAV and MOM have similarly disrupted mainstream narratives by developing women's leadership and making demands for positive social change.

CHAPTER 2

Building Women's Leadership
Interrelationality as Feminist Praxis

It is in collectivities that we find reservoirs of hope and optimism.

ANGELA Y. DAVIS, FREEDOM IS A CONSTANT STRUGGLE.

You didn't see me on television, you didn't see news stories about me. The kind of role that I tried to play was to pick up pieces or put together pieces out of which I hoped organization might come. My theory is, strong people don't need strong leaders.

ELLA BAKER QUOTED IN ELLEN CANTAROW, *MOVING THE MOUNTAIN*

In our movements, it often seems like people are struggling to be seen, to be somebody, to meet with someone who is somebody. . . . All of us need to figure out something that we're kind of good at or willing to study up on, something we feel passionate enough to make a long-term commitment to and dig into material work.

DEAN SPADE, "NOW IS THE TIME"

Introduction

Women's leadership has been an ongoing issue within social movements, as men often are given outsized credit or tend to hold more formal leadership roles, but both MOM and CAAAV have sustained a commitment to developing women's leadership because it figures largely in their aims for social change. MOM and CAAAV provide an opportunity to consider women's leadership in more complexity, given that their members found their way into groups that emphasized collective struggle grounded in shared identities and concerns. Women were able to take on key roles in mixed-gender groups seeking racial and class justice because both organizations valued interrelationality (reciprocal support among community members) and acknowledged the existence of complex intersectional identities. Through activist narratives and the politics expressed by both groups, members identify as part of a "collective self" that emphasizes a shared identity (as Asian, Black, Puerto Rican, a South Bronx resident, low income) and learn frameworks that "help reinforce and promote the collective welfare of the group" (Uhl-Bien, "Relational Leadership Theory," 259). Their capacity to simultaneously claim and mobilize around shared identities while embracing diversity within their own groups as well as in their alliance work aligns with the queer political sensibilities outlined by scholars like Cathy J. Cohen. This approach to activism that whereby one seeks to radically improve life in one's communities through collective effort rather than by following a few charismatic leaders encapsulates the queer motherwork style.

As left-oriented groups, both MOM and CAAAV support a leadership approach that "is not only transformational in style, but has economic, political and social transformation as its goal" (Antrobus, "Transformational Leadership," 50). These aims, which align with long-standing practices of social movements, can be put into conversation with the individual narratives of activists. Activists' stories provide a sense of how participation in social justice work facilitated their sense of themselves by illuminating how oppression works and the potential of collective action to challenge the status quo. Through their activism, they gained the necessary "recognition and affirmation [that] strengthens one's identity as a leader . . . [and also] helps to sustain the level of interest and fortitude needed" to fight for social justice (Ely, Ibarra, and Kolb, "Taking Gender," 476).

Because both groups prioritize women's participation, gender-related issues and efforts to address sexism across contexts have been crucial to their work. Notably, both groups see gender justice as a commitment to inclusion and so do not call for ostracizing those within their communities who perpetuated sexism and heterosexism as a result of their socialization. Activists in both organizations have sought out ways to improve dynamics within them and to encourage an intersectional approach to social justice work. These values continue to be primarily tied to women's gender socialization, thus explaining the centrality of women in both groups (Kaplan, *Crazy for Democracy*, 6–7). In this chapter, I draw on an intersectional framework to illuminate how complex identities inform women's entry into social justice leadership.

As many scholars' work has established, women of color's social justice leadership in the United States is vibrant and multifocal and crosses a range of social issues (Thompson, "Multiracial Feminism"; Giddings, *Sword*; Ransby, *Ella Baker*; Hewitt, *Southern Discomfort*; White, *Too Heavy*; Orleck, *Storming*, 2005; Guglielmo, *Living*; Carroll, *Mobilizing*). Of particular import here is the extent to which women of color embrace collective agency. This appreciation of networks and knowledge of the process of coming into community-based activism is based in a critical relationship to U.S. liberalism and its centrality to mainstream feminism and scholarship; CAAAV's and MOM's histories play out lessons taught in the work of Ella Baker, Yuri Kochiyama, Grace Lee Boggs, and other leaders (Davis, *Meaning*, 132; Ransby, *Ella Baker*; Kao et al., "Tributes").

Kochiyama was a mentor for CAAAV activists owing to her embrace of radical politics, and United States Black civil rights activists and Latin American radicals served as role models for MOM's activists. These legacies demonstrate that social movement power comes from lifelong engagement and support of the development of activist generations rather than the cultivation of individual status. A more robust history of social justice movements emerges from recognizing that the movements in which activists take part are composed of wider networks of participants, some of whom may not receive recognition or take on formal roles and who may move in and out of activism during their lifetimes. The politics of CAAAV's mentor Yuri Kochiyama, as Diane C. Fujino observes, "promoted the collective leadership abilities of ordinary people. She rejected the charismatic leader as an individualistic and masculinist model" (Kao et al., "Tributes," 28). In this chapter, I further explore how identity-based activism provided a platform for women of color's development, both personally and politically. The selected narratives offer insight into the differing trajectories that together make up the histories of CAAAV and MOM, as well as the broader movements to which they contributed in their first decades.

Intersectionality has increasingly become central to work across academic disciplines and holds particular import for the analysis of women of color activists' histories. It provides a framework for understanding the desire of groups like the Combahee River Collective to situate its politics in multiple social identities rather than one. Kimberlé Crenshaw draws on intersectionality to address the failure of legal analyses to account for the experience of Black women as both Black individuals and as women. She famously uses the metaphor of a car accident at an intersection to describe intersectionality; there are often multiple interacting factors that cause such an accident, just as discrimination has different sources ("Demarginalizing," 149). Reflecting on how the term has developed over the past two decades, Patricia Hill Collins and Sirma Bilge provide a working definition in their 2016 book *Intersectionality*:

> Intersectionality is a way of understanding and analyzing the complexity in the world, in people, and in human experiences. The events and conditions of social and political life and the self can seldom be understood as shaped by one factor. They are generally shaped by many factors in diverse and mutually influencing ways. When it comes to social inequality, people's lives and the organization of power in a given society are better understood as being shaped not by a single axis of social division, be it race or gender or class, but by many axes that work together and influence each other. Intersectionality as an analytic tool gives people better access to the complexity of the world and of themselves (2).

There have been recent concerns that the term's broad usage cuts it off from its origins in the political critique of Black feminist thought, and, at times, about the way it is taken to be simply a methodological intervention (Alexander-

Floyd, "Disappearing Acts"). Nikol Alexander-Floyd defines intersectionality "as the commitment to centering research and analysis on the lived experiences of women of color for the purpose of making visible and addressing their marginalization as well as an ethos of challenging business as usual in mainstream disciplines' habits of knowledge production" (9). This definition emphasizes the importance of structural analysis rather than objectification. Jennifer C. Nash also notes a tendency to treat Black women as a monolithic category. She points to intersectionality's attempt to draw "attention to difference while also strategically mobilizing the language of commonality (however provisional or tentative that commonality might be) in the service of constructing a coherent theoretical and political agenda" ("Re-Thinking Intersectionality," 8). In seeking to be attentive to difference while creating a common cause, one may indeed end up relying on simplistic and potentially reified understandings of subject categories. Nonetheless, as Jasbir Puar notes, "to render intersectionality as an archaic relic of identity politics . . . partakes in the fantasy of capacity-endowed bodies bypassing the possibility that for some bodies . . . discipline and punish may well still be the primary mode of power apparatus " ("'I would rather,'" 63). As is seen in the case of MOM and CAAAV's histories, intersectionality holds a critical place for work that recognizes the continued salience of identity categories in everyday life. Intersectionality is a key component of queer motherwork as it provides the grounds for naming activists' capacity to claim identity along with a sense of shared struggle across communities of color.

Intersectionality is a crucial facet of queer motherwork for two key reasons. First, a recurrent theme in the activists' stories told here is their understanding of themselves and their community's experiences in terms of multiple axes of oppression—e.g., both sexism and racism or both poverty and racism. To ignore this would be to ignore their own accounts of themselves as well as their efforts to challenge single-issue approaches to identity-based politics. Second, an intersectional analysis—based on a recognition that identity categories are simultaneously imposed and incomplete while also a critical means of social organization, repression, and resistance—is necessary to elucidate CAAAV's and MOM's members understanding of their identities, experiences, and relationships, their broader communities and worlds, and their activism. Their commentary demonstrates that they have been driven to activism by a mix of feminist, racial, and class-based values and commitments. As a result, they have reimagined and participated in feminist activism without compromising other core commitments. They led and joined efforts to respond to police brutality and incarceration, just as they fought for domestic workers' rights and against pollution that drove South Bronx residents into hospital emergency rooms. By refusing to separate these issues, they embrace the totality of their heterogeneous communities and in the process emphasize women's continuing outsized role in managing and addressing critical needs, thus enacting queer motherwork.

The histories of both groups' members elucidate the tensions that can arise for individuals who have been socialized into a narrow set of marginalized identities when they seek out others who share their experiences. Claiming a politicized identity is not a simple process, and both groups offered members the opportunity to embrace multiple identities at once. In their stories, CAAAV activists often mentioned their struggles over how to embrace an Asian identity in the face of limited, flat stereotypes. Overarching concerns with racial and class justice, the lack of which was the source of their marginalization, pulled MOM's members together across identities. As MOM and CAAAV activists became catalyzed in their work, they found themselves part of a broader community of social justice activists in New York and globally. For many, participation in movement work produced a sense that their lives were entwined in powerful ways, even if these ties were subject to fraying. This interrelational understanding contrasts with an approach that values individualism, which has the effect of underestimating the contributions of the many, and that regards poverty as stemming from personal or communal failure (Allison, "A Question"; Nash, "Feminist Critique"; Schwartzman, *Challenging Liberalism*). Multiple narrators in this chapter point to a sense of isolation or individual suffering, whether as an exploited worker or as a public housing resident. Through their social justice engagement, they discovered that collective identification and action could help them and others facing similar challenges. This shift in their perspective allowed them to see that their marginalization had its roots in structural inequalities and a lack of equal opportunity. Members of MOM and CAAAV came to understand that their struggles were the result of larger forces requiring a movement response built from the grassroots of their communities. My usage of the word "queer" in *queer motherwork* thus highlights the political nature of activists' analyses and actions in their accounts of the sociopolitical context of their interventions.

The range of individuals' own comfort level with the attention I bestowed as a participant observer as well as their career paths (a number of members moved into and out of the groups, others maintained formal ties as regular volunteers or board members, and still others collaborated through their work in allied groups), dynamics within each organization, and journalists' coverage skew how activists' participation is documented in my book. I highlight the work of activists who were active as I conducted my ethnographic research, who made significant contributions to the day-to-day operations of each group, and who were willing to participate in formal interviews. I draw on additional documented materials ranging from oral histories to media coverage to further address key concerns raised by this chapter's focus on women's leadership.

Both groups have prioritized the work of women from their founding. CAAAV's roots were in the Organization for Asian Women and other groups that responded to anti-Asian violence in the 1980s. Asian women were aware that they were at risk of violence and took on the responsibility of defending their community, much as Ida B. Wells did in response to anti-Black lynching (Giddings, *Sword*) and lesbians did in response to the HIV/AIDS crisis (Hutchison, "Lesbian Blood Drives"). CAAAV's thirtieth anniversary celebration, held in May 2016, brought together many of the women who had played key leadership roles in the organization and highlighted their contribution: "CAAAV's legacy and history has been built by the remarkable women who built the base, developed leadership of community members, developed strategic campaigns, coordinated direct actions, showed up in solidarity for others, and built the infrastructure of the organization" (caaav.org/30th_anniversary/caaav_30th .html). The celebration underscored the connection between each woman's contributions and the growth of CAAAV over the three decades.

MOM incorporated an emphasis on motherhood as a basis for action into its name. This approach reflects its origins in educational justice, as cultural gender norms across communities typically assign women the responsibility of ensuring the success of their children. In the South Bronx, this role is foregrounded, as the area has high rates of women as single heads of household. Moreover, the organization was willing to support and build up women as leaders within the group owing to the legacies of Black and Puerto Rican women's activism (Enck-Wanzer, *Young Lords*; Gallagher, *Black Women*).

The practice of putting women in central positions proved to be an accepted norm in MOM and CAAAV, underscoring each group's commitment to marginalized community members and to working toward the greater good. Both organizations provided women with space in which to learn more about their own capabilities and the structural inequalities informing their lives and communities. As housing organizer Nova Strachan noted, MOM was where she first learned about the 1970s Bronx fires and about how the poverty her community experienced was rooted in governmental and business exploitation and neglect, including the racist redlining practices that limited federal and private investment in the area (interview with author, March 5, 2008; see also Glazer, "South-Bronx Story," and Gonzalez, *The Bronx*, 111). When Sung E. Bai, CAAAV's executive director from the 1990s into the 2000s, joined CAAAV, she had already begun her racial justice journey; the group offered a space where she could fully explore what it meant to be an Asian woman and begin organizing to address the issues she was learning about in graduate school. Both CAAAV and MOM helped members in a variety of ways, from introducing them to canvassing by taking them around to knock on doors to invite community members to events to getting them to reanalyze the histories of their communities and their own lives.

Entry Points

Women's paths into CAAAV and MOM varied based on whether they were already activists. Some women came into these organizations already identifying with some pieces of the groups' work, such as racial justice activism, and were drawn to the work that centered on their identities and concerns. Others entered first through projects that addressed their immediate needs, such as domestic workers' rights or housing justice, and in time found that the organization provided support and a space to develop their racial, gender, and/ or class consciousness as well as gain or practice organizing skills. The demographics of each group are distinct but women activists' experiences in both of these groups illuminate the possibilities of shared participation in community action as well as a need for spaces where such women are engaged and supported. MOM and CAAAV made it possible for women to claim their own identities, histories, and futures and to reject gendered, racial, classed, and other forms of oppression. Moreover, their personal journeys were intertwined with their work to empower their communities, as they addressed threats from racial violence to gentrification.

The Organization for Asian Women, the precursor to CAAAV, was cofounded by Kazu Iijima. Iijima had a long history of New York Asian American activism, including cofounding the Japanese American Committee for Democracy that was established in 1940 as the Committee for Democratic Treatment for Japanese Residents in Eastern States (Robinson, "Nisei in Gotham," 587). The group was committed to antifascism as well as to Japanese-American solidarity (it supported the West Coast internment as part of the antifascist war effort while also welcoming residents resettling in New York), and it also faced challenges when it came to engaging with other communities of color. Interestingly, a 1943 newsletter editorial articulated a politics that shared much with CAAAV's priorities at the end of the century: "We [Japanese Americans] must be in the forefront of the struggle against any act of racism, There can be no compromise on this score. ... It is singularly absurd, and totally fascistic, for Japanese Americans to practice Jim Crow and anti-Semitism at the same time they profess Americanism—or democracy" (Robinson, "Nisei in Gotham," 591).

Iijima went on to found the more militant Asian Americans for Action in 1969, an organization that was explicitly pan-Asian, inspired by the Black Power movement, and that sought to address the racist and imperialist facets of the Vietnam War (Omatsu, "Kazu Iijima," viii). She joked that her cofounding of Asian Americans for Action with Minn Matsuda came out of a discussion between "two old ladies sitting on a park bench." Iijuma proved to be an important bridge through her radical and intergenerational work. Bette Yee, a longtime CAAAV activist of Chinese descent, decided to look into the Organization of Asian American Women because of Iijima, as she explained in an February 26, 2012, interview with Cynthia Lee for the Brooklyn Historical Society's *Crossing Borders, Bridging Generations* oral history project. She bumped into Iijima after she moved to Brooklyn, and Iijima told her about the Organization for Asian American Women. Yee's initial reaction to Iijima was "Wow, how interesting. Radical Chinese women" (40). While Iijima was Japanese American and the group was pan-Asian, Yee was particularly drawn to the possibility of connecting with people who shared her political, ethnic, and gender identities. The slippage between her own identity as Chinese and the broader range of Asian women in the group suggests how deeply she desired a space in which she could explore being a radical Chinese woman as well as points to the implicit East Asian ethnocentrism within CAAAV's history. It is noticeable that the list of the thirtieth anniversary women leader honorees reflects an East Asian majority, although diversity in membership in the 1990s and 2000s and CAAAV's projects addressing South Asian and Southeast Asian communities have mitigated this bias. Yee's participation in Asian American movement work affirmed her ethnically specific claims of identity as Chinese while allowing her to connect with other Asian Americans across communities who had experienced racism (Okamoto, "Toward a Theory"; Wei, *Asian American Movement*; Aguilar-San Juan, *State*). In the Organization for Asian Women, CAAAV identities viewed as disparate—in mainstream representations of radical politics, in Asian American communities, and within feminism—could be claimed.

Future CAAAV executive director Sung E. Bai first became politicized in the 1980s as an undergraduate at Cornell University. She had been born in New York to Korean immigrants and moved around during her childhood to different parts of Queens, the Bronx, and Long Island. As a young woman, she felt lost, disconnected from both herself as an Asian woman and her college educational experience, as she navigated mixed ethnic and classed social milieus in the New York area. In a fortunate turn of events, she found a new community, political perspective, and an outlet when she came across a campus anti-apartheid protest during the beginning of her second semester: "I'm walking along campus and I hear all of this screaming. . . . At the time I had no idea what a protest was. . . . I was curious though, and I was witnessing a civil disobedience where people were being dragged and arrested and put onto school buses" (interview with author, June 5, 2008). The passion of the activists and the injustice of apartheid drew her quickly toward political activism:

> I kind of just got involved, not as a staunch member of any one particular organization. . . . [I] ended up getting arrested for civil disobedience for the first time as part of this. . . . I was learning more and more about what was happening in South Africa, which was really the first time I was thinking about anything out-

side of the United States or outside of myself in a lot of ways, and so I just really got completely drawn into it.

Challenging apartheid began to open up an understanding of the broader world of injustice and activism for Bai, as it did for many young people in the 1980s. It provided an opportunity for her to learn about and respond to global white supremacy and mobilizations by people of color. Moreover, it provided her with an outlet for meaningful engagement, allowing her to experience the powerful and risky practice of civil disobedience.

Bai found herself moving between the highly visible white students who were mobilizing and Black advocates from the university and community who had been doing anti-apartheid work for a long time. After a difficult year, she transferred to nearby Ithaca College. As she remembers: "I just picked classes that had to do with race and politics. . . . I started getting more involved in people of color-issues." Bai found herself drawn to coalitional work challenging the xenophobic English-only movement that attacked bilingual provision of basic services such as education and sought to enact English-only laws or make English as the sole official language of the United States. This xenophobia, while primarily stemming from anti-Latinx sentiment, also threatened Asian immigrants and tapped into broader anti-Asian bias that rendered Asian Americans perpetual outsiders.

Out of these efforts, Bai became part of a community that enabled her to more fully participate in social movement work and to better understand her own experiences as an young Asian American woman. As she recounts, a more senior Asian college woman introduced her to intersectionality as a means of addressing violence: "She was part of that generation of Third World–minded, conscious folks. . . . I was of the 'race first,' that was my consciousness. And she was schooling me on gender, basically, and talking about how you can't say that it's race. It's not a race-versus-gender issue, but that you needed to look at both at the same time." This revelation opened up the possibility of combining antiracist and feminist work. Bai organized an Asian American women's support group that engaged racism within mainstream feminist organizing efforts such as Take Back the Night. After graduation, she came back to New York City and began volunteering as a hotline advocate and volunteer trainer, then as a board member, for the New York Asian Women's Center, an organization addressing violence against Asian women. As she became steeped in this work, she realized she wanted to get involved with more direct grassroots activism, and she established connections with other activists, such as Ai-jen Poo, who would join CAAAV as a domestic workers organizer and become a national leader on issues related to care work.

Bai's journey to working with CAAAV was not seamless. She remembered encountering CAAAV activists during the early period of her activism in the city, but she thought the group focused solely on "anti-police-brutality work, and I figured, 'Oh, that's not really my thing, I'm really looking at violence against Asian women issues.'" She was not aware of the broader work CAAAV had been doing to counter anti-Asian sexism, such as the campaign against the Lambda Legal Defense Fund *Miss Saigon* fund-raising event. "I didn't have any other analysis, it was pretty narrow," Bai reflects. As she had done when she was introduced to a gender analysis in college, Bai opened herself up to challenging her assumptions about what Asian women's organizing could be. She decided to volunteer with CAAAV and in time started CAAAV's Women Workers Project, which melded her desire to explicitly address Asian women's issues with CAAAV's commitment to working-class Asian struggles in New York City (CAAAV, "CAAAV Launches"). This project enabled her to more fully appreciate her shared oppression with woman workers as an Asian woman, despite her class and educational attainments.

For Bai, becoming part of CAAAV required that she challenge herself to make connections with women that mainstream feminism did not address owing to its tendency to singularly focus on women's experiences of gender-based oppression. Bai first sought out interactions with a part of the Asian community with which she was less familiar but felt a kinship with as an Asian American. From there, she began tackling issues such as police brutality within the Asian community—particularly within the Cambodian community that CAAAV worked with in the Bronx. This activism returned her to the issue of state-sponsored racist violence that had first drawn her to activism during the antiapartheid movement. At the same time, she was working with a group that was open to engaging with questions of violence against women, which in time allowed her and her colleagues to establish CAAAV's Women Workers Project, an organizing effort that would spawn Domestic Workers United in the 2000s. Through her work as volunteer, organizer and executive director Bai was empowered to become an advocate for both a diverse New York Asian community and New Yorkers of color more broadly.

A group interview with members of the Women Workers Project that CAAAV organizer Carolyn De Leon arranged for me demonstrated the range of ways women connect with activism and that their engagement may ebb and flow. The project succeeded because Filipina domestic workers are a significant part of this workforce in New York and other global cities. The kind of domestic worker advocacy CAAAV engages in is a form of queer motherwork because it takes into account the fact that workers' care work complicates simple notions of family, belonging, and love and the fact that the exploitation of domestic workers can negatively impact their communities and families. Activists' stories revealed that although they shared an identity as Filipina domestic workers who had migrated across the globe and ended up in New York City, they each had distinct stories. Nita Asuncion joined the project after the group offered to help her fight back against her abusive employer. Josie Rumna joined because of her friendship with Asuncion. As she recalled, "I'm involved with the women's organization because we help our friend, Nita Asuncion, for her case that her employer abused her every day" (interview with author, March 21, 2009). Even though Rumna had limited time off from her work and despite the commute she had to make to attend meetings, she went the extra yard to participate, as she wanted to improve working conditions and appreciated that CAAAV members were fighters. Star Dungo learned about the group through its community outreach at her church. While she was drawn to the group, her engagement fluctuated: "I stopped for a long period of time. And then they sent me a letter for a mammogram [a service provided as part of CAAAV's health fairs] and it lift my spirit again and join them again." Her experience emphasizes the importance of the group presenting her with opportunities that struck her as meaningful, such as a health fair where she would receive services. Star maintained her friendships with other Women Workers Project–connected Filipina/o domestic workers and believed that the work the group undertook was particularly important for workers at risk for abuse because of their immigration status. Friendship proved to be a critical component for another member, Inday Baldivia. She had known Carolyn De Leon since the early 2000s. By 2004, she had friends working in the industry that needed help and reached out to Carolyn. She found that CAAAV was able to provide the advocacy they needed to stand up to exploitative employers. The Women Workers Project offered hope to this group of women and to women they connected to based on their national identity and their migration and work status.

The path into organizing and making a new home in New York was similar for MOM activists. Wanda Salaman, MOM's executive director beginning in the 2000s into the present, migrated from Puerto Rico to the Bronx as a child. She initially became involved with youth organizing through the local church and sports. A charismatic youth, she was able to negotiate with her local parish priest to get snacks for her and her friends as well as government cheese for her family in exchange for bringing her friends to church to listen to the priest's sermons. She remembered, "I would be making deals with this guy about what I want and the other kids from the neighborhood would follow the stuff that I was doing. So it was like, easy for me to do that with him. So I made demands and he would follow them and I realized, 'Oh, this works!'"(interview with author, July 15, 2008). From her youth, Salaman demonstrated a particular acuity for drawing people together and for figuring out what she could parlay for the given group she was representing. After she joined a local baseball team, she met a community elder, Astin "Jacob" Jacobo. He connected her to the Bronx

Youth Community Organization through which she was introduced to housing organizing work. She remembered the group's work in the late 1980s: "We used to do like this tenant patrol.... And one time I remember, there was no water in this building. And it was cold. We had to do a line, organize a line so people could pass buckets of water ... to put in the boiler so they could have heat that day." While her family was able to secure good housing with proper services, Salaman recognized both that other Bronx residents were struggling and that through organized effort they could address these dire conditions. The work of her group resulted in the building becoming a cooperatively owned building, showing her the power of tenant organizing.

As a young adult, Salaman continued to participate in organizing. She left the Bronx Youth Community Organization and became an advisor for the Fordham Youth Project, which organized "community rallies, a paper, and all that other stuff." She earned her associate's degree working in clerical jobs during the day and pursued activism at night. Eventually, she became an office manager for the Northwest Bronx Community and Clergy Coalition. Sister Pat, whom Salaman had known when Sister Pat was an organizer for the Crotona Community Coalition, told her about Mayor Rudy Giuliani administration's plans to cut youth programs. Salaman recalled, "So then one day, she was like, so 'If I organize the youth will you help me?' ... I was like, 'Alright, Sister Pat, I will work with you.' So we did it as a partnership." Salaman worked with her old mentor Jacob along with Sister Pat, eventually confronting Mayor Giuliani and his youth commissioner at City Hall about the cuts to youth program funding (Hicks, "Budget Battleground"; McKinley, 1994). The bulk of the cuts to youth programs were scrapped the following month thanks to these efforts and negotiations with city council leaders. That she was able to mobilize her community and address the mayor helped Salaman see that she had what it took be a paid organizer, a path that would in time lead her to MOM and eventually to becoming its executive director.

Salaman moved easily into activism as an adult, having been involved as a youth, and her strength as an organizer came from the support of a mix of mentors from Sister Pat to Jacob in her community. For Bai, the path into CAAAV was slower, as her focus was on Asian women's issues and CAAAV's was not. But she was eventually drawn in because she was open to the group and sensed that the work they were doing with Southeast Asian communities mattered to her as someone invested in Asian issues. In contrast, Filipina domestic workers were eager to join CAAAV, because they had urgent needs that the group could address. Activism helped these women become agents in their communities. In the next section, I consider what engagement with MOM and CAAAV offered in terms of leadership development by looking at the types of work they did and skills they gained.

Organizers from both groups utilized a mix of leadership approaches mentors taught them with tactics they learned from collaboration within and across organizations. As MOM and CAAAV were left groups with a racial justice orientation and a history of women's leadership, activists in each group had significant room to take an approach that aligned with their own personality and the culture of the group. While activists did not always share the same priorities or cultural capital—they had, for example, differing levels of formal education and different ways of presenting themselves—the range of women that participated in both groups demonstrates an openness to styles that did not conform with gender, raced, and classed norms that have often confined women's leadership opportunities more broadly. Community outreach and direct action protest were part and parcel of the work for members and staff; thus, CAAAV and MOM activists sought to both build community and work with actors tackling the issues. The women grew through their work in these groups, uncovering strengths and learning organizing tools. Popular representations of activism do not often dwell on the process by which activists learn the trade. They navigated challenges, at times failing to adequately work through them and at other times succeeding and thereby strengthening their bonds. In my interviews with activists, they emphasized the positives of their organizational experiences, and so I learned about these kinds of challenges more through my ethnographic work. For example, informal conversations with CAAAV activists in the late 2000s suggested that there were some interethnic tensions, as self-identified "brown Asians"—Filipina and Southeast Asians—felt that they did not have the same cultural capital as their East Asian counterparts in the organization. In MOM, white staff members came in and out of the organization rather quickly, and members had differing class and cultural backgrounds that sometimes caused social distancing. Confronting barriers to committing to struggles that face strong opposition as well as finding ways to become more confident and comfortable within the contradictions of social justice organizing are critical aspects of the work of both groups. A queer mother-work approach that does not downplay complexity and that emphasizes mutual respect enabled activists to find their power as activists. In particular, an embrace of interrelationality and sense of shared struggle allowed activists to continue working together despite tensions or take a step back from their organization when they were frustrated and to not engage in pettiness that could negatively affect the group, its members, and their works.

Born and raised in New England (born in Boston, growing up in New Hampshire), Bette Yee eventually moved to New York City as an adult, drawn to its diversity; as she recalled in her interview with Cynthia Lee, "I never knew what it would feel like to be part of a Chinese community" (38). While Yee "knew community organizing a little bit," she was "more on the secretarial side." With CAAAV, she noted, "we were really forming committees, and we were trying to get people to speak, and ... trying to do outreach" (42). So, the group enabled her to take her engagement to a new level and see herself as a full actor in the movement's work. She observed that activist work was better able to flourish in New York City as opposed to her native New Hampshire because "there were more resources here.... Asians ... who you could access that had resources"(42). The group was able to grow during the mid-1980s by using its connections, which made it possible, for example, for it to access event spaces for free or reduced cost to promote its work. Notably, for Yee, the group in its early stages allowed participants to develop their own politics. As she reflected, "We would laugh at ourselves. We call ourselves radical, and yet we really don't know how to be radical"(42). As they journeyed toward becoming radical New York Asian women, CAAAV women would build an organization that was stalwartly antiracist and that would stand through waves of anti-immigrant, anti-Asian, and anti-Black violence in the city and beyond; this organization's work would respond to police shooting deaths, the U.S. wars in Iraq and Afghanistan, and hate-based crimes.

Inday Baldivia summarized the value of CAAAV's Women Workers Project for her personally and other Filipina domestic workers. "You feel secure in spite of hardship....So many times domestic helpers are being oppressed." But "knowing that there is CAAAV that you can lean on" helps; "somebody's there to help you" (interview with author, March 21, 2009). Baldivia emphasized that the organization's help with abuses that workers experienced on the job was particularly important, as such workers struggled with isolation. Many domestic workers, she pointed out, "are alone here. They have no family. They by themselves.... It's hard to be alone in this country." Nita Asuncion noted that the Women Workers Project spawned the Domestic Workers United, a multiracial organization that would be central, in turn, to the formation of the National Domestic Workers Alliance in 2007. When asked about moving from the Filipina-centered approach that defined the Women Workers Project to the multiracial approach that characterized the Domestic Workers Alliance, the group replied that it did not find the shift to be an issue. As Asuncion explained, "We like it because they are friendly and welcoming and different." Having built trust with one another as Filipina workers, they found engaging more fully with women workers across backgrounds to be exciting. She described the union's approach as "always teaching one another to work on and to move forward even how quiet you are.... They educate you how to speak out." The Women Workers Project and the growing Domestic Workers Union empowered them to fight back against their silencing (Hondagneu-Sotelo, *Doméstica*; Constable, *Maid to Order*; Boris and Parreñas, *Intimate Labors*).

MOM's Wanda Salaman recalled that her mentor, Jacob, pushed for her to pursue an organizing position for the Crotona Community Center. Jacob was a Dominican immigrant who became known as the "Mayor of Crotona"; he worked as an elementary school custodian while also serving as an influential community advocate (Pace, "Astin Jacobo"). Center leaders were particularly drawn to Salaman because she had grown up in the area. Her training often confirmed that the methods she had been using as novice activist were appropriate: "Learning the words and terms was like, okay so that makes sense. It's what I was already doing" (interview with author, July 15, 2008). She had already been exposed to the practices and logic of community organizing, but at the center, she learned the mainstream terminology of community activists. Salaman benefited more from her mentors and interactions with community members than from formal community organizing training: "The discussion I had with [community members like] Miss Ella about her experiences or Thelma's experiences is when I was learning." Rather than participate in training sessions, she wanted "to leave and do this in the neighborhood or do something else." The knowledge that Salaman received from the men and women of her own community was critical for her. She also noted the mismatch between her values and the Alinsky-style organizing that was white- and male-dominated, which meant there were "no discussions of race, class, or gender." As she recalled, "My being around white folks was mostly through my organizing. . . . It was funny, the housing and neighborhood organizers would be white but the youth organizer had to be Black or Latino or whatever." Salaman's critique resonates with antiracist and feminist ones that resulted in new styles of organizing being developed in the 1990s (Sen, *Stir It Up*, xlix–lv). Salaman sought to challenge the assumptions of white organizers whose activism focused on themselves instead of her community's people and their concerns. Her understanding of community needs as structured by race, gender, and class resulted in Salaman taking a mentoring approach with new organizers: "I just wanted them to do the job, and I want the best for them and for my neighborhood," adding that the experience "might be nice on their resume, but while they're here, they better do the shit that I need to do in my neighborhood." Salaman was recruited to work at MOM because her mentors and other colleagues from groups like Crotona Community Coalition recognized that she would be a good match for the organization given her roots in the community and experience with grassroots organizing. She welcomed the opportunity, starting out as a paid housing organizer, because the organization had women of color mentors like Mili Bonilla that Salaman was interested in working with. Described as "one of the best organizers I know" by renowned feminist and antiracist activist Rinku Sen, Bonilla succeeded in building the base for MOM and went on to became an advocate in New York City government: first, she served as New York City Council speaker Melissa Mark-Viverito's community engagement liaison and then as the chief of staff for Diana Ayala, the city council member for District 8 (an area that includes East Harlem and the majority of the South Bronx). Bonilla is particularly savvy about how to effectively empower community members, deploy tactics to engage stakeholders, and garner media attention, which in the case of Salaman proved critical to her growth as an organizer (*Stir It Up*, 96).

For Maria Rivera, MOM staff member, the organization opened up the possibility of addressing the issues that the South Bronx had struggled with beginning in the late 1970s. In particular, the feeling of abandonment as the city disinvested in the area took its toll on the sense of community that she initially felt as a child arriving from Puerto Rico. She remembered that when her family came to the South Bronx in the early seventies "you was able to leave your doors open, your windows open. You could sleep in your fire escape" (interview with author, July 13, 2010). By the end of the decade, buildings burned, including the one in which her family lived. She noted that "back then I didn't know if there was a movement to help the community to fight for social justice or fight for them to lower your rent, for the pollution, for illnesses or whatever the case may be." As a participant in the city's "workfare" Work Experience Program, she was sent to MOM because she had clerical skills as a bilingual GED holder and her asthma prevented her from performing groundskeeping work in New York parks, a common placement for the Work Experience Program clients. As historian Tamar Carroll describes, the program "created a new class of low-paid city workers without benefits, masked in a moralistic rhetoric of public assistance recipients' obligation to society" that was characteristic of the 1990s national bipartisan embrace of the defunding of public assistance (*Mobilizing*, 340–41). Rivera's mix of skills and health challenges opened the door to this atypical placement where she would be exposed to a critical perspective that countered the assumptions that undergirded the program.

At MOM, Rivera learned the basics of social justice organizing as she worked. Rivera remembered that while she was in the office, she saw MOM staff and members preparing for a rally.

> I was like "What's this? Where they going to with all of them signs? And you're going where? To a rally? City Hall? For what? ... Social justice. What's that?" Well, that's fighting for the issues the community has. . . . I saw the rallies and the marches and the press conferences. . . . Little by little getting all this knowledge of what's this, what's that, because I really didn't know.

Her entry into MOM put Rivera into direct contact with organizers such as Wanda Salaman and housing organizer Nova Strachan, who welcomed her questions and explained both the concepts that drove the organization's work and the tactics its members used in their campaigns. Eventually, Rivera began to help Strachan by "translat[ing] from English to Spanish, Spanish to English" and taking part in door knocking and phone outreach, summarizing her conversations with residents as "'Come on. Let's work on a campaign, because this landlord in X place is not giving heat and doing the repairs, so we're going to do a campaign.'.... And that's how I started." Salaman, who was now the executive director of MOM, was able to get Rivera a position with another human service nonprofit, the Federal Employment and Guidance Service, which also placed workers at MOM. Rivera helped them gain the skills she had acquired during her time at MOM. "People get together and things get done" is the message Rivera took away from her experience of working with these workers on MOM's successful campaign to close the New York Organic Fertilizer Company. The satisfaction she received from participating in MOM's work contrasted with the anguish she felt as she watched her neighborhood's struggles when she was growing up and as she faced the challenges of seeking employment through the city's public assistance program.

Women activists across CAAAV and MOM worked both with women who shared their identities as women of color and with women who did not, as in the case of domestic workers who joined with women of different races and from different nations. Instead of compelling these activists to prioritize their identity as either a woman or as a person of a color, both groups treated these identities as inseparable. As Salaman argued, mentoring from other women of color was critical. She recalled telling an early boss that "I need a mentor that I can relate to. So I'm gonna talk to Mili," the Puerto Rican cofounder of MOM. At MOM, she said, "I could look for women of color. And I told my boss, 'I need a mentor but I don't want you'"(interview with author, July 15, 2008). She respected Blanca Ramirez, another MOM organizer, and she remembered that "my whole idea was that coming into MOM was that I wanted to work more with Blanca and I saw her as like a mentor type of person." She sought a space where class and race issues were approached intersectionally by women of color. CAAAV similarly provided a space in which Asian women were able to help each other become radicalized and support one another as they organized to fight abuses that particularly targeted women like themselves. These practices of mentoring grounded in shared identity as women of color drew on their lived realities. As they navigated the intersections of sexism, racism, and other categories, activists learned from each other's experiences, challenges, and survival strategies. These dynamics contrasted with the tendency among men and/or white activists to downplay their own participation in or the ways they benefited from systems of oppression, which resulted in their being distanced from the daily struggles of women of color activists. Both groups' unapologetic valuing of women-of-color-centered mentoring reflects the radical potential of queer motherwork.

MOM and CAAAV are organizations that recognize that their members' and communities' multiple identities and challenges are central to their activism. MOM helped women develop a political understanding of the deep poverty and related social issues that the South Bronx grappled with. They named the classed and raced components of inequality in public housing and in the local schools. They reframed the problems facing their community by uncovering the economic, social, and political factors that gave rise to them. In a January 26, 2008, power analysis training session centered on their environmental justice campaign, MOM members read out loud and discussed two quotes. The first was from Martin Luther King Jr.'s "Where Do We Go from Here?" speech:

> Now power properly understood is nothing but the ability to achieve purpose. It is the strength required to bring about social, political and economic change. . . . [T]here is nothing wrong with power if power is used correctly. . . . Now we've got to get this thing right. . . . What is needed is a realization that power without love is reckless and abusive, and love without power is sentimental and anemic. Power at its best is love implementing the demands of justice, and justice at its best is power correcting everything that stands against love. And this is what we must see as we move on. (41–42)

The second was from Frederick Douglass's speech on West Indian emancipation:

> Those who profess to favor freedom and yet depreciate agitation, are people who want crops without plowing the ground, they want rain without thunder and lightning. They want the ocean without the roar of its many waters. This struggle may be a moral one, or it may be a physical one, and it may be both moral and physical, but it must be a struggle. Power concedes nothing without a demand. It never did and it never will. (367)

The group considered how love and dedication could help build a stronger campaign in the community. The quotes prompted a discussion about the successes and failures of the civil rights movement. An older man recalled how people's power was actualized during the 1960s, and a younger woman commented on the time that it took to pool resources and fight racism. It became clear that MOM members were frustrated by the lack of active support for their work from their friends and neighbors in the community. As Tanya Fields, future founder of the BLK Projek and Libertad Urban Farm, noted, "Most people don't realize when they don't make a decision, you are making a decision." To illustrate her point, she argued that local politicians did not feel a need to engage nonvoters, so not voting was a critical choice that created a vicious circle.

As the day progressed, participants began to define power by identifying words they associated with it. Thinking about money, clout, people, knowledge, communication/dialogue, and union, they struggled to come up with a definition that took into account both the power they had that was manifested in their advocacy initiatives and their lack of control over the decisions that were being made in and for their community. Two women members, Pamela and Terry, emphasized the communal aspects of power, maintaining that MOM had the potential to help the community affirm its right to exercise control over its environment. In the end, the group defined power as a way "to effectively build and utilize resources to control the destiny of our community, while simultaneously gaining name recognition and thus becoming a community resource." MOM's members thus emphasized finding a balance between building community support for their activities and spreading the word about the organization so that they might more effectively negotiate with decision makers. As Black and Puerto Rican women, MOM's women members had to navigate racist and sexist stereotypes that framed them as irrationally angry and undeserving of respectful engagement. Activities such as the quotation discussion provided an opportunity to own the right to critique without apology the issues that their community confronted.

Many CAAAV activists came of age in communities where they were isolated as Asians, while others grew up in more robust Asian communities in New York or their home countries. Across these different upbringings, they struggled to find their own power in the face of mainstream stereotypes that emphasized their outsider status and assumed their passivity. Taking to the streets to protest *Miss Saigon* provided an opportunity to challenge such assumptions directly (Eng and Hom, introduction). MOM and CAAAV provided a space where activists could find a new way of connecting to others as well as to themselves.

Working with other women who shared at least some of their identity-based experience proved to be critical for some activists. In reflecting on her time with the Organization for Asian Women and CAAAV in the 1980s, Yee emphasized how much she valued the common stories of other members and the opportunity to share her story "with somebody who understood my experience" (interview with Cynthia Lee, February 26, 2012, 41): "I never experienced that before. . . . So all of a sudden, I really have a group of people who really, I would talk politically with, I didn't have to . . . watch what I was saying, and as a matter of fact, they were so much more radical than me. It was . . . scary" (41).

Through her participation in CAAAV, Yee was able to explore her politics more fully, but she also pointed out how this intense engagement was challenging in such a small group. "I was with them for all this time," she noted, and "it got to be a very small community" (41). The issues CAAAV addressed left its members feeling emotionally drained, and the way significant bonds were made or broken as friendships developed or ended echoes many feminist activists' experiences with social justice collectives.

Bai's experience of coming into CAAAV and becoming its executive director after working as a volunteer and then paid organizer gave her the time and space to grow. She reflected, "I've come a long way in terms of . . . self-awareness, my presence and my interactions with people, how much I can influence people or a space by virtue of my attitude, my energy," although she also expressed a wish she "had that heightened awareness early on rather than later . . . in terms of class politics, in terms of politics of gender" (interview with author, June 5, 2008). As she continued pushing the boundaries of her political analysis around gender, class, and race, Bai became more aware of intersecting social identities and power dynamics within her organization and ally groups. Bai mentored the next generation of activists, as Shaun Lin, an intern, noted in an interview: "She really went out of her way to take me under her wing. . . . She used to drive me up and we'd have basically deepening ideology discussions on the way up to the office" about such topics as LGBTQ rights and heterosexism (interview with author, August 26, 2008). While Lin was able to build his knowledge through these conversations, CAAAV also provided its members with formal opportunities to learn, including leadership training courses, an introduction to community-based organizing, and courses on current issues. For example, immigration reform emerged at the forefront of New York State and national politics in the mid-2000s, and activists from groups such as CAAAV participated in marches and rallies to show support for immigrant rights. Josie Rumna, a Women's Workers Project member and domestic worker, remarked, "another thing that I really admired was every time there's a meeting here, there're invited people that will help you to learn what's going on about immigration" (interview with author, March 21, 2009). This mix of formal and informal engagement enabled CAAAV to maintain and promote its vision of women-centered racial justice.

Women who were part of MOM were likewise able to gain the skills and confidence they needed. Salaman's experience of bringing her organizing experience and self-awareness to her work contrasted with that of other women who were new to activism. Nova Strachan gained a new frame of reference for exploring questions of social justice when she moved from being a Work Experience Program worker to housing organizer. MOM, she noted, provided "a good education":

> You're learning things you ain't never even think you'd be bothered with or want to know because it's boring or whatever the case is. But this is the stuff you should know. So they also exposed me to the politics and things of that nature

that before I didn't really care about or felt it didn't affect me in no way. So I didn't care, I didn't see it. (interview with author, March 5, 2008)

Growing up in the 1980s and 1990s as a resident of public housing, Strachan did not see the point in knowing who her councilperson was or what rights she had as a tenant. Working with MOM, she learned about how activists used this information to address the problems in their community and become invested in the connections she made with activists and with other members of her community. Moreover, she gained access to formal training through her participation in Social Justice Leadership's Activate!, a now defunct program, organizing fellowship programs; this training broadened her skills, teaching her strategic planning and self-care as an organizer. Like Strachan, Rivera found that MOM offered her a new way of being in the South Bronx. She reflected:

> Movement, movement. You know, to move this from here to here. I didn't see it like a whole bunch of people moving—and even saying the word I just get all these other thoughts in my head, like "Yo, it's a very powerful word, 'movement.' I'm going to move this issue from here and fight for it and put it somewhere else or fix it or whatever it may be." So I'm grateful for Mothers on the Move. (interview with author, July 13, 2010)

Rivera understood movement to be key to bringing about change that had been previously unimaginable to her. She emphasized that change required many people coming together and working in tandem rather than as individuals and that her capacity to "move an issue," such as by challenging the acceptance of trucks roaring down residential streets and getting responses from city officials, gave her a sense of power that was new. MOM gave Rivera a sense of possibility for the future of her community.

CAAAV and MOM promoted a model of leadership that emphasized women's agency in social justice movements, not simply their roles as supporters or beneficiaries. Rather than providing a path into activism only for women with relative class and educational privilege, each group has sought to build its campaigns and programming in a manner that is inclusive of the community members who have lived with the issues they seek to address. The capacity for women of color to simultaneously express and be engaged as both gendered and racialized people, putting intersectional theory and politics into practice in a manner that did not require they cut off or simplify who they were, provided both organizations with members who were capable of connecting around difference while pursuing issues that were personally significant to them. This dynamic context ensured that both groups could grow projects. In the case of CAAAV's Women's Workers Project, the input of participants revealed new opportunities. Nova Strachan's firsthand experience with life in the

South Bronx's public housing ensured that as a MOM housing organizer she would more fully connect with community members. In striving to empower people at the heart of issues they are organizing around, both groups' efforts have manifested the elements of queer motherwork that highlight identity, collaboration, and community. The next chapter turns to how women led each group in developing approaches to organizing around these critical issues.

CHAPTER 3

Organizing Strategies
From the Streets to the Courts

I don't think there will ever be a time when people will stop wanting to bring about change.

YURI KOCHIYAMA, QUOTED IN MARIA IU, LETTER

Freedom is always and exclusively freedom for the one who thinks differently. . . . Only experience is capable of correcting and opening new ways. Only unobstructed, effervescing life falls into a thousand new forms and improvisations, brings to light creative force, itself corrects all mistaken attempts.

ROSA LUXEMBURG, "THE RUSSIAN REVOLUTION"

In Image 2, victorious MOM activists pose with New York's Department of Environmental Protection commissioner Emily Lloyd outside her Park Slope, Brooklyn, brownstone home on October 27, 2007. Despite her broader work to improve water quality and improve environmental practices in New York, Lloyd had twice refused MOM's requests for a meeting to discuss their concerns about air quality in the South Bronx (Mackenzie "Sweet Smell," 6). In response to her unwillingness to engage them as her constituents, they traveled the fifteen miles by bus from the South Bronx to speak with her at home. Making their case face-to-face, MOM members called on Lloyd to acknowledge their concerns over the Department of Environmental Protection's plan to expand the water pollution control plant in the South Bronx and its failure to address poor air quality in their neighborhoods. Lloyd came out of her house to speak with MOM activists, posing with them for photographs, and agreed to schedule a sit-down with the group.

Their decision to pursue a meeting with Lloyd and refusal to be ignored are representative of tactics activists in immigrant communities of color have adopted to move their organizing agendas forward. Addressing the complex root causes of environmental racism, housing inequality, and the exploitation of domestic workers that are at the heart of CAAAV's and MOM's agendas called for multiple and overlapping strategies. Such a multifaceted approach was also

IMAGE 2. MOM activists with Department of Environmental Protection Commissioner Lloyd (second row from bottom, center), October 27, 2007. Photo by Wanda Salaman.

necessary because of the uncertain efficacy of any one method, whether that was grassroots organizing or seeking relief through the courts (Jung, King, and Soule, "Issue Bricolage"). In the case of MOM's efforts to engage Lloyd, official forms of communication failed when she rejected their requests for meetings or that she participate in their community forums, so they adopted a more confrontational approach that ended up working. Fighting for the future of their communities, MOM's and CAAAV's queer motherwork has been expressed as a dynamic fierceness that defies respectability politics and that is not constrained by expectations of political purity.

Flexible tactics like those used by MOM to get Lloyd's attention were key to its ability to carry out long-term campaigns that secured concrete wins for their communities. During the 1990s and 2000s, CAAAV and MOM ceased being largely single-issue organizations and developed sophisticated campaigns that engaged the many different parties—community members, employers, public officials, media, and allied organizations—that had a stake in the issues the organizations were addressing. MOM and CAAAV had to employ unique and overlapping approaches to get these different parties to participate in the work the organizations engaged in and to take seriously their demands for change. This chapter explores three key methods that both groups used: direct outreach, protest and theater, and legal strategies. CAAAV and MOM activists walked through neighborhoods in the South Bronx and Manhattan, climbing up and down stairs in rental and public housing buildings, and handing out fliers in parks, as they sought to build the base of their organizations and connect with New Yorkers impacted by environmental racism and failing housing policies. From these ties, they garnered the power to carry out protests as well as form networks with other activist groups to use social justice–themed theatrical productions to convey their message to a broader range of New Yorkers. Finally, they pushed for the enforcement of existing laws and new legislation to force action from local authorities that too frequently ignore the needs of the marginalized constituencies that are the heart of MOM's and CAAAV's communities. Their shifting, multiple methods provide the opportunity to develop a fuller explication of the limitations of and opportunities for enacting queer motherwork.

The organizing discussed in this chapter centers immigrant and U.S,-born women of color, not because I assume their identities are homogenous but because their oppression has been determined by commonly held sexist, racist, xenophobic, and classist ideas about women, people of color, immigrants, the poor, and service workers. The assumption that these people, by virtue of their identity or status, are not able to form their own analysis of their lives or change their society continues to inform mainstream representations of their histories and communities. They have suffered from labor stratification, the failure to protect workers' rights and guarantee safe housing, and a dominant culture that frequently refuses to acknowledge their claims to dignity and resources. MOM and CAAAV activists brought together groups of people to protest their marginalization and push back against status quo inequities. Their life histories offered them a wide range of local and global perspectives that proved critical to this work. They grounded their activism by combining their stories with insights they gleaned from seeing the continuities between their current struggles and the longer histories of oppression and social justice organizing. Both groups used the sharing of their own experiences and what they learned through workshops, political education, and engagement with other groups to build this sense of a bigger picture. Their larger understanding of both community and root causes of injustice is at the core of queer motherwork as a form of praxis that centers on connection and refuses to apologize for desiring a better world. CAAAV and MOM activists' efforts drew on both their creativity and their traditional organizing skills in a vibrant mix of long-term planning and improvisational social justice work.

This dynamism suggests that social justice organizations cannot be simply understood in terms of radical versus liberal politics and service-providing versus advocacy work binaries. Much like queer conceptually and politically challenged binaries, queer motherwork, emerging out of feminist-of-color thought and praxis, challenges assumed neat boundaries of political practices. As Chicana feminist theorist Chela Sandoval argues in *The Methodology of the Oppressed,* women of color necessarily move "between and among" four feminist oppositional ideological approaches—equal rights/liberal (women and men are the same), separatist (women and men are essentially different), supremacist (women are better than men), and revolutionary (women are a divided class)—rather than subscribing to an either/or approach (56–58). This political approach acknowledges "simultaneous existence of contradictory and complementary positions," according to Anna Sampaio ("Transnational

Feminisms," 188). Thus, activists have developed a holistic model that recognizes shifting practices, flux within organizations and political contexts, and louder and quieter emphases of particular identities and that more fully engages organizations' histories and contributions. As leadership and membership shift and the political environment changes, organizations adapt in ways that may appear contradictory but that in fact demonstrate the dynamism necessary for a group's long-term survival.

Direct outreach and base building, methods that seek to ensure a growing organized constituency, are critical components of community organizing (Sinclair, McConnell, and Michelson, "Local Canvassing"). In this section, I examine efforts by CAAAV and MOM activists to reach disenfranchised workers and residents and document how their tactical flexibility contributed to their success. CAAAV initially struggled to find ways to reach low-wage, Asian, immigrant women workers, but it gained traction after it began to collaborate with and address the needs of domestic workers. Although domestic workers are often considered "unorganizable," CAAAV found a way to recruit them into a growing labor rights movement (Shah and Seville, "Domestic Worker Organizing"; Middaugh, "Lessons"; Smith, "Organizing"). MOM activists sought to empower South Bronx tenants to organize and claim their rights in the face of increasing attacks on public housing. Such attacks were occurring across the city and the country, and in response, activists formed the national organization the Right to the City Alliance, which both CAAAV and MOM joined. Canvassing was a particularly effective means of outreach for CAAAV and MOM because they understood the keys to making it work. Canvassing is a good way to addresses geographically contained issues, and the members of the community who are canvassed get a sense of activists' capabilities by how well they respond to the concerns that they voice during such encounters. MOM and CAAAV thus were able to attract new members as well as to convert activists into organizers. These recruits were sincerely interested not only in their own communities' issues but also with those of others. Their insights have proved necessary to shifting the attention of MOM and CAAAV from broad concerns about inequalities to the specific concerns of their communities. Through their canvassing, MOM and CAAAV learned how community members themselves think about these issues, what they want, and what they are willing to do to fight back.

By the mid-1990s, CAAAV activists had come to recognize that violence Asians in New York City faced affected the day-to-day life of community members. In the wake of this recognition, they decided to change CAAAV's organizing structure. As Sung E. Bai recalled, "We were organizationally talking about the kind of work we were doing up until then and so we had one structure of these ethnic-based communities, so the Korean community organizing committee, etcetera" (interview with author, June 5, 2008). Working within ethnic boundaries seemed to provide a way to navigate the complications of a pan-Asian politics. Not only did the ethnic identifications of CAAAV members vary widely, but so did their socioeconomic status and the languages they spoke. At the same time, the issues that CAAAV activists were drawn to and their embrace of an Asian American movement politics that deliberately forged connections across experiences challenged them to question this single-ethnicity approach. They recognized that it was time to attempt to develop projects that could cross ethnic boundaries and that were focused on interethnic community needs. Out of these discussions, they also determined that it was important to be, as Bai put it, "really thinking about how to be more long term in our thinking, and so not jumping from project to project, or campaign to campaign, but really about building community power." CAAAV activists reframed their anti-Asian violence work so that they were not only reacting to anti-Asian violence and anti-Asian cultural representation but also focusing on developing empowered and resilient communities by adopting a cross-ethnic approach to their work, despite the distinct histories and identities of each Asian group. This move toward a holistic consideration of their community's diversity reflects a step toward queer motherwork.

This organizational shift made it possible to initiate a project that would address Asian immigrant women, who were notoriously exploited in a range of professions in the city. Despite CAAAV's hopes for working cross-ethnically, the isolation Asian immigrant women experienced as they entered New York's informal labor markets beset the project in its early stages. CAAAV's Bai and Alexandra Hye were studying sex work in their graduate program at Columbia University and became aware of the Rainbow Center (rainbowcenterus .org/english/aboutUs/history.html), a Christian faith-based organization working with Korean women, primarily former wives of U.S. veterans (Moon, *Sex*). Bai and Hye recognized that this was a constituency that was not being organized, in contrast to garment workers, and that the concerns of sex workers were connected to larger struggles to address violence against women. They wanted to engage and empower Korean sex workers around their labor rather than provide services to them as the Rainbow Center did (Limoncelli, "Trouble with Trafficking"; Hye, "From a 'Short Time'"). The Women Workers Project, as Bai summarized, " was really different from the way that other projects came about." The project would become one of CAAAV's most significant contributions to labor organizing in the twenty-first century, helping establish Domestic Workers United and the National Domestic Workers Alliance (Boris and Nadasen, "Domestic Workers"; Poo, "Twentieth-First Century"; Obias, "Organizing Domestic Workers"; Solis, "Remarks"). Violence toward and the exploitation of immigrant women was a focus for the life of the project, although its focus would shift dramatically and core members would turn over from the 1990s into the 2000s.

The Giuliani administration's project to "clean up" New York, beginning in 1994, embattled sex workers even more. The efforts to close strip clubs and related venues prompted dancers to turn to paid sex acts and also pushed many workers indoors to avoid the police (Alexander, letter to the editor; Jacobs, "Shuttered Clubs"; Murphy and Venkatesh, "Vice Careers"). In addition, the Giuliani administration unevenly targeted segments of the sex work industry, focusing on Asian massage parlors. The resulting economic strain caused many Asian sex workers to become migratory; they often would spend a few months in New York and then seek work in other parts of the region. This moving around created a deep obstacle to any effort to build a base for organizing, Bai noted. The climate of fear created by the administration's focus on Asian sex workers also made it hard to address issues such as criminalization, violence, sexism, and xenophobia that CAAAV activists were interested in.

Women Workers Project activists began their outreach to sex workers by posting fliers written in English, Korean, and Mandarin. The fliers addressed workers who might "have questions about: POLICE RAIDS; VIOLENCE at WORK; NEW CHANGES IN THE LAW." The project was introduced as a way "for Asian Women working in massage parlors, to come to improve their working and living conditions. . . . We are interested in talking to you about important issues in your lives and your experiences with police raids or arrests." The flier's text also connected the project to the broader work of CAAAV: "We are part of an organization who has been fighting police abuse for 10 years. We have a lot of knowledge about police procedure, the legal system, and violence against Asian women in new york [*sic*]." While seeking to overcome the barriers to organizing sex workers and demonstrate its background in tackling criminal justice system challenges faced by Asian New Yorkers, the Women Workers Project also anticipated and addressed other concerns. It emphasized that "*we are not a religious, legal or government organization*" and "we are *not* advocating for women to leave this work." Sex workers were encouraged to attend organizing meetings as well as English classes and to make use of translation services that CAAAV provided for women "in the business."

Despite these efforts, however, few sex workers came to Women Workers Project meetings. However, even with the challenges the organization faced in drawing sex workers to the meetings, it did not give up; it advertised widely for an Asian immigrant women's health fair and got better results. As Bai explained, "We started off [the project] with this broad analysis that it's about the informal service industry, what would unite Asian immigrant women in different industries is that they're all part of this economy that's changing." Women working in a range of fields were experiencing hardships, and so they decided that "we'll cast the wide net, so the health fair, you know, advertise it to everybody people working in nail salons, to sex workers, to domestic workers, whoever and let's see what happens." This approach proved successful.

At an August 26, 1998 meeting, the Women Workers Project decided to formally redirect its focus from sex workers to nail salon and domestic workers. In addition to using activities like the health fair to try to make connections, they also continued their own research into working conditions faced by individuals in these occupations. A handwritten note in the CAAAV papers from the meeting agenda indicates that they thought that nail salons were home to workplace hazards that should be pursued with the federal government's Occupational Health and Safety Administration. Here, too, the project focused on an industry in which Asian, specifically Korean, women were concentrated and faced conditions that undermined their health and their rights as workers. The project's "Political Analysis of the Korean Owned Nail Salon Industry in New York" presented members' rationale for focusing on this area, including the labor abuses identified by project volunteers and staff. By the mid-1990s, the report noted, "80% of all Korean owned businesses in New York [were] nail/beauty salons.... [There were] approximately 24,000 Korean owned nail salons in the city." Despite a media frenzy regarding public health risks for nail salon customers in New York, there was little interest in what nail salon workers themselves were dealing with, which included wage exploitation and health dangers from the toxic chemicals used in salons.

The Women Workers Project again found itself hamstrung by dynamics that had undermined organizing efforts in the past. One problem was that the group wanted to protect salon workers from health dangers, but it also feared that more government regulation could pose a risk to undocumented immigrant women. This challenge limited the extent to which the group was able to work with local or federal agencies to enforce existing industry-specific protections for workers or establish new ones, and it also narrowed its focus to organizing documented workers. The group did continue providing health services to undocumented workers with a partner organization, Nodutdol for Korean Community Development, a progressive Korean antimilitarism group. Another challenge the Women Workers Project faced is that in explicitly foregrounding a class-based analysis, the direct antagonists of Korean nail workers ended up being Korean business owners. Nail salons reflected the growing economic diversity among immigrants between 1960 and 2000; this shift undermined cross-class solidarity within the broader Asian American movement, as some Asians had financial, educational, and familial resources while others came to the United States as refugees or low-income workers (Liu, Geron, and Lai, *Snake Dance*, 162). Organizing nail salon workers would raise questions about the well-being of women working in Asian-owned and -managed businesses generally. In the case of sex work, the high-profile violence against workers by customers and the Giuliani administration's antagonism to the industry muted the problem of intraethnic discord; however, activism on the part of nail salon workers brought to light conflicts between Asian owners and their employees. Scholar Miliann Kang describes this dynamic as both a form of "labor paternalism" and "labor maternalism," as workers deeply connected with the idea of employers as coethnic providers of community support even as their labor was exploited ("Manicuring Intimacies," 223–24). As a result of these tensions, project activists were again unable to find a way to develop a successful strategy for bringing in workers. However, during these first two stages the health fairs the group sponsored for all Asian immigrant women workers drew in Filipina domestic workers that took the project in new directions.

These health fairs were spaces in themselves where CAAAV activists could meet and connect with Asian workers, but the outreach that led up to them also depended on networking. Carolyn De Leon, a former Filipino Women Workers Project organizer, recalled her first encounter with CAAAV's activists. She saw "a group of Asian folks doing outreach in the park, someone with a flier . . . for a health fair." She was immediately interested, and she recalls that "[I] showed up [to the health fair] with my two friends [who were also domestic workers]. I was right away helping . . . [to] set up and serve food." She came away from the fair thinking "Oh, I'm finally going to find something to do, really useful . . . I can do something better on the weekend, when I'm on a day off" (interview with author, July 21, 2008). Her interest in finding a meaningful activity for herself in her free time reflected the isolation many domestic workers experienced as well as the pain caused by the stigmatization of their work. Her inclination to bring friends with her to the event demonstrated her instinct for networking that is critical to organizing efforts. De Leon would use her passion to recruit other domestic workers in the city's parks and to help to build the Women's Workers Project as it expanded into Domestic Workers United.

Outreach in the city's parks was an important facet of the project's growth, as De Leon's experience attested, since it made use of spaces in which domestic work is publicly visible. Such public spaces are where domestic workers typically make acquaintances and friends, as they sit together, talking and interacting with the children in their care. In urban areas around the globe, domestic workers often congregate in public areas while working and on their days off (Constable, *Maid to Order*; Hondagneu-Sotelo, *Doméstica*, Parreñas, *Force*; Das Gupta, *Unruly Immigrants*). These interactions in public spaces contrast sharply with domestic workers' experiences in the homes of their employers, where they were isolated in high-rise apartments, far from their friends.

De Leon canvassed in the same parks where she used to regularly discuss the challenges of domestic work in the United States with other women. Together, they would try to find solutions to problems such as inadequate pay and lack of time off. De Leon herself had experienced such problems when she first came to the United States to work as a live-in domestic worker in the New

York suburbs. Her employers, whom she had first worked with in Hong Kong, violated the contract conditions they had agreed on, and she demanded that they cover basic needs such as winter clothing. Fortunately, De Leon made contact with a Filipina domestic worker friend she had also met in Hong Kong. Her friend showed her how to use public transportation to get from the suburbs to Queens, where New York City's Filipina/o community is heavily concentrated. By connecting with an existing network of Filipina domestic workers for support, De Leon was able to quit a job that had isolated her in suburbs and find a more satisfactory one in the city as a live-out nanny. She became a member of a vibrant Filipina/o community, and she built friendships with women like her who had left the Philippines, seeking work abroad to support their families back home. She also met other women who had migrated from places like Trinidad, Tobago, and Jamaica in search of similar opportunities. Some workers joined the Women Workers Project as a result of these kinds of outreach efforts and positive word of mouth. They tended to be drawn to the project either because of their own negative experiences as workers or those of their friends; they were also attracted by the concern for and sense of responsibility to women of their community that defined the project.

The skills needed to establish rapport with workers during outreach were on display during a 2008 canvassing trip with De Leon and CAAAV's Shaun Lin to Manhattan's parks to recruit more members to the project. De Leon was able to approach and chat with some domestic workers, while she could do no more than hand a flier to others. Frequently when canvassers approached domestic workers walking with children, their young charges would demand attention from their caretakers, and so the domestic workers would not be able to engage with them. Workplace barriers to discussing workers' experiences and potential interest in collective action is a general problem that activist often encounter in organizing. However, there is a qualitative difference in the domestic work setting because it is a hybrid of public and private work that is commonly surveilled. Caregivers are not easily able to take a break from their responsibilities to talk. New York mothers also share these spaces, chatting and enjoying a sunny day in the park with their children while simultaneously overseeing the labor of other women. Despite these challenges, the Women Workers Project was able to build on the networks that domestic workers themselves had, and by 1999, CAAAV had hired De Leon to reach out to Filipina workers as well as Afro-Caribbean women workers. De Leon had already built friendships with workers across national and racial lines as a worker, and this network was an asset that the previous iterations of the project lacked. Her hiring demonstrated that CAAAV understood the importance of incorporating workers themselves as organizers; breaking down the barrier between Asian activists and Asian workers was critical to the success of the project.

The Women Workers Project's incorporation of Afro-Caribbean women transformed it into a multiracial undertaking. This effort began with outreach in Brooklyn and the establishment of a Caribbean workers steering committee in 2000. As organizing continued, it also incorporated preexisting organizations such as Andolan, serving South Asian domestic workers, and Damayan, serving Filipina domestic workers, setting the stage for the development of Domestic Workers United that included workers from a range of countries into one organization and existed alongside the Women Workers Project until it came to an end in 2009. As a result of Domestic Workers United's work, changes were made to city and state law that guaranteed workers' basic rights such as paid overtime and paid days of rest. Activists drew on the diverse and diffuse nature of this community of workers to bring to life organizing that would not only change the laws in New York but be an important piece of the reemergent domestic workers' rights movement in the United States and internationally.

While CAAAV's Women Workers Project initially had trouble using outreach tactics to build its base, MOM's housing campaign was more readily able to draw on these traditional practices in its work with a community that was identifiable and had a century's legacy of tenants' rights organizing (Lawson and Naison, *Tenant Movement*; Gold, *When Tenants Claimed*). The ongoing challenge in this arena is to convince residents that organizing provides an opportunity to truly change their circumstances. Public housing in the United States has been notoriously neglected since the 1960s, and residents' sense of what was possible was undoubtedly shaped by broader discourses that tended to dismiss their homes as part of a failed social program. MOM's housing organizer Nova Strachan canvassed South Bronx public housing buildings with the goal of getting residents to become active participants in the broader debate over the future of public housing and to address specific concerns in their buildings, such as lack of repairs or garbage pickup.

In both the cases of MOM and CAAAV, canvassing proved particularly successful when at least some of the organizers shared the experiences of the people they were trying to organize. Strachan could speak to residents about her own challenges, since she had lived her entire life in Bronx public housing. For example, she recalled, "I have bullet wounds in my door. Like somebody was shooting in the hallway, so it's like the bullets didn't go through my door but they bounce off the door.... And I feel like I'm the only person with this on my door, like I feel kinda funny" (interview with author, March 5, 2008). Strachan understood firsthand how the failure of the New York City Housing Authority (NYCHA) to maintain its buildings made her feel insecure and isolated as a tenant. Similarly, De Leon was able to cultivate a network as well as speak with workers with a familiarity about the unique benefits and drawbacks of care work by drawing on her own experiences as a domestic worker. Both groups struggled but ultimately succeeded in using the time-consuming and energy-taxing work of canvassing to bring in the most important people to their cause—the people harmed by the problem at hand.

Another way CAAAV or MOM activists canvassed was by inviting community members to protests and performances. The opportunity to witness or participate in a public action showed potential members what CAAAV or MOM could do with their help. Activists utilized both direct action and theater in order to communicate with a broader public audience about their causes, and their campaigns often combined elements of each approach. Public protests served to escalate the call for a response to the concerns voiced by community members. Public confrontations further heightened the stakes by making visible the realities of inequality that often remained hidden. Activists used theater to construct narratives that could cultivate empathy for a cause not only among an immediate audience but also across a broader public when performances garnered media attention. All of these approaches helped fuel the energy of MOM and CAAAV, and they gave members multiple outlets in which to publicly express why they chose to act and refused to accept inequities such as environmental racism and the exploitation of domestic workers. These public acts enabled MOM and CAAAV activists to loudly claim their own dignity and to shame actors who failed to recognize and respond to their demands.

MOM activists long used direct action to counter public officials' and business leaders' reluctance to take their concerns seriously. For example, they turned to direct action to address the dangers that truck traffic posed to the safety of their community. After six-year-old Crystal Vargas was killed by a commercial truck on Longwood Avenue while bicycling near Fufidio Triangle's sidewalk in Hunts Point, MOM and other community groups sought to force New York's Department of Transportation to properly regulate the heavy commercial traffic in Hunts Point and pushed for truck route changes, more barriers, speed bumps, and law enforcement. MOM produced television public service announcements, directly confronted government officials and representatives, and undertook its own study of truck traffic in the area. Throughout this campaign, MOM worked extensively with other Bronx organizations such as Sustainable South Bronx.

The coalition struggled to get a response from city officials (Portlock, "Asthma"). The critical target of their campaign was Department of Transportation (DOT) commissioner James Kilkenny. Kilkenny repeatedly refused to meet with the group and then once he did finally come to the South Bronx, he ended up openly dismissing activists when he abruptly ended the visit in response to the forthrightness of MOM members, accusing them of being rude for demanding accountability for community safety (Rutenberg, "Big Trucks"; Transportation Alternatives, "DOT"). At the same time, the department was hoping to increase routes through Hunts Point and was planning to conduct a citywide truck study to see if that was feasible. Facing outrage from MOM and others, it backed off this plan, but troubles continued). On October 21, 1998, Kilkenny finally met with MOM members and reportedly promised to make marked improvements to the area's roads; the city would install "permanent speed humps and traffic medians by Spring 1999" and "look into other traffic calming devices from signs to wider corners" (Tri-State Transportation Campaign, "Bronx Neighborhood"). But by December, Kilkenny had gone back on his word and said he had made no such promises or set any deadlines and refused to meet again with MOM (Tri-State Transportation Campaign, "Bronx Neighborhood"; Transportation Alternatives, "DOT," 14).

In response, MOM escalated its tactics from direct action to symbolic street theater. Members marched on his Westchester Square office carrying "a Grinch doll labelled 'Kilkenny' and an effigy of a child on a stretcher" and shouted that he was the "Grinch that stole our safe streets" (Corey, "Popularity"; Transportation Alternatives, "DOT," 14). The mainstream cultural referent of the Grinch worked to present the community's perspective that safety was rightfully theirs and that it was the department's inability to control truck traffic that was stealing the lives of members of their community. By January, the department had installed a temporary median at Spofford Avenue in an effort to diffuse the situation. Although city representatives resisted working directly with community groups such as MOM, the organization had succeeded in forcing authorities to do something about the dangerous traffic situation.

MOM used similar tactics to raise awareness about the stench emanating from a fertilizer and waste treatment plan, New York Organic Fertilizer Company, that was operating with expired permits. Local coverage of MOM protests included an article by Jose Acosta titled "Aquí no hay quien respire" ("Here, No One Can Breathe") for *El Diario/La Prensa* (4). The article title picked up on the dire nature of the conditions that MOM activists were protesting, while a *New York Times* piece by Tina Kelley titled "What Stinks? The Mourners Wore Hazmat Suits" highlighted the dramatic tactics utilized. Some MOM members wore white painters' jumpsuits to simulate hazmat outfits or carried large mock inhalers made out of tubing, bottles, and poster board, and almost all wore face masks or respirators to connect the fumes with the neighborhood's shockingly high asthma rates. I was given the honor of bringing along a papier-mâché skunk made by MOM's Barbara White. The skunk was a gentler representation of what MOM's Lydia Vélez described to reporters as an "un olor a huevos podridos, cuerpos putrefactos" ("an odor of rotten eggs, putrefying bodies"). Finally, MOM members carried a couple of small black wooden coffins to visually present the lives that were threatened by poor air quality and the inability of residents to enjoy the limited public spaces in their neighborhood.

While MOM's protests outside the gates of the fertilizer company drew media attention and provided members with an opportunity to express their outrage publicly, the tactic failed to evoke a direct response from management.

MOM continued to build support for its campaign through its Toxic Bus Tours in 2007 and 2008 (mothersonthemove.org/coverage.html). Other organizations had successfully used this strategy, for example, groups on Chicago's South Side in the 1990s (Kaalund, "Witness to Truth," 79). Through the bus tour, MOM activists were able to play on ideas of tourism while taking outsiders into their community. The August 17, 2008, tour that ended at company headquarters garnered coverage from the local television station NY1. It highlighted MOM's complaints, which prompted the Department of Environmental Protection to state publicly that it would investigate the smell (NY1 News, "Activists"). As Carmen Silva recalls, the bus tours brought targets of the campaign into contact with the odor that residents complained about. "Everyone was covering their mouths" in response to the smell (Mackenzie, "Sweet Smell," 6). These approaches helped convince outsiders that neighborhood residents were not exaggerating about how bad the stench was. Political theater is a different format from protests for conveying a radical political vision for the future and for exposing the underlying practices that produce inequality (Colleran and Spencer, introduction, 3–4). MOM's embrace of artistic expression provided it and its constituents with a way to offer a more nuanced and reflective representation of the issues, albeit for smaller audiences, than is possible with brief and blunt protests that usually reach a wider public.

In the photo from *Exit Cukoo*, Latinx playwright and actress, Lisa Ramirez hoists a baby carriage above her head as she stands on a rough cement block with a river behind her. The image was used in fliers for a Domestic Workers United fund-raiser performance of her one-woman play *Exit Cuckoo* (Domestic Workers United, "*Exit Cuckoo*"). The play dramatizes the range of workers in New York City's care industry. Mimicking the Statue of Liberty's pose, Ramirez represents both employers and domestic workers involved in care work. On one hand, for U.S.-born employers, her stance may invoke maternal strength or independence; on the other, her standing on a rough block of concrete emphasizes the devalued physical labor immigrant domestic workers engage in and the isolation they face. As Domestic Workers United and DataCenter reported in 2006, 99% of domestic workers were foreign-born and 76% were not U.S. citizens ("Home," 10). By mimicking the preeminent symbol of the United States' promise of freedom and a prosperous future, Ramirez foregrounds the unfulfilled expectations of these immigrants for political incorporation and upward mobility while simultaneously emphasizing domestic workers' role as protectors of U.S. children. The play challenges the long-standing silence around domestic work by left-wing activists and scholars, some number of whom rely on domestic workers for social supports such as daycare (Kvist and Petersen, "What Has," 200). Ramirez brings this erasure to light and provides a valuable resource for domestic workers' rights activists seeking to reach new audiences.

The play's intent is to "expose the myth of motherhood," and its intended audience is domestic workers and their political allies. *Exit Cuckoo* not only presents Ramirez's perspective on New York's domestic work industry but also has served as an outreach and fund-raising tool for Domestic Workers United. In a scene late in the play, Ramirez's character Lisa witnesses a Domestic Workers United march. She is carrying a sign that reads "Free Domestic Workers! End the Slavery!" and is welcomed into the protest by other marchers. Ramirez thus suggests the importance of organizing (and support for organizing) as a means of addressing the inequalities the audience has witnessed throughout the performance. This interest in engaging both consumers and laborers creates a productive tension in Ramirez's work, a tension that is likewise evident in broader efforts by DWU to gain support for the Domestic Workers Bill of Rights campaign, which sought to improve labor standards without alienating and demonizing employers themselves.

Ramirez's performance in the play attempts to bridge the practice of domestic work across time with the disparate experiences of workers and employers. As the play concludes, she acknowledges that at first "I thought that becoming a nanny was the worst thing that had ever happened to me," owing to the denigration and frequent isolation of this work. But, she reflects, "I think about the park benches I've sat on, the different homes I've been in. . . . I think about all the women who know nothing about each other except that one has money, the other one needs it and there is a child in between them that needs to be taken care of." Marking this dynamic that pits women against each other, she adds that there is another option. She recounts the words of a domestic worker activist: "'We can do together what we cannot do alone.' . . . If I could just get them all in the same room . . . 'Talk!' I'd say. 'Tell her what you told me. Talk . . . tell her what you told me. TALK!'"(42). Throughout the play, Ramirez dramatizes key components of problems with the industry as well as the first steps needed to facilitate change. Moreover, she refuses to displace herself from these tensions; she acknowledges that she struggled with internalizing the devaluation of domestic work. She also emphasizes that women can develop better ways to address the issues at play in contemporary domestic work through supporting Domestic Workers United.

Different organizations made efforts to ensure that workers had the opportunity to see the show. In March 2009, in advance of the play's off-Broadway premiere in March 2009, the Working Theater, which is home to "high-quality affordable theater for and about working people," sent out a call for outreach in an email to an NYU gender studies list:

> Domestic workers are currently pushing for a "Domestic Workers Bill of Rights." . . . We are determined to share their story with as wide an audience as possible. Working Theater is offering free tickets to domestic workers across the city. . . . We will spend a couple of hours approaching nannies and caretakers in public parks, daycare centers and gymborees around the city[;] . . . help us reach out to domestic workers and offer them the opportunity to see theater that is for and about them.

Working Theater offered free tickets for volunteers as well, underlining its mission while utilizing Domestic Workers United's central outreach tactic. This approach enabled the theater to affirm its solidarity with the union, actively promote the Domestic Workers Bill of Rights, and reach out to domestic workers who might not otherwise be able to see *Exit Cuckoo*. An outreach effort on the morning of Thursday, April 9, 2009, brought together two Working Theater staff members, Laura Carbonell Smith and Mark Plesent, and a couple of volunteers from local colleges and universities. Domestic workers in Madison Square Park in Tribeca and another park along the Hudson River were enthusiastic about the idea of the play and the free admission being offered them, even if they did not think they would be able to attend. The outreach recalled the roots of Ramirez's own relationship to domestic work and organizing. Erline Brown, a domestic worker who had been a leading member of Domestic Workers United since 1999, noted in an outreach meeting held at the Working Theater on March 30, 2009, that she had met Lisa Ramirez at a park in Tribeca when both were working. She observed that one way to draw workers to the play was to highlight the fact that "this is a woman you probably know" and that the play reflected their common experiences. The performance thus not only offered a critique of the status quo but also served as a platform for activists to connect with workers as well as employers.

Theater also gave community members an opportunity to directly interact with their representatives and the broader New York community, empowering them to take the stage and use art to reflect on their experiences. MOM's Nova Strachan, for example, performed in the 2011 revival of *Pins & Needles*, a Broadway musical comedy revue written and performed by International Ladies Garment Workers' Union members between 1937 and 1941. This musical revue was initiated by Brooklyn's Families United for Racial and Economic Equality (FUREE), pronounced "fury," a close ally of MOM and CAAAV, and in collaboration with the Foundry Theatre. *Pins & Needles* provided an opportunity for Strachan to train and perform and also demonstrated MOM's commitment to Strachan's personal development. Moreover, the performance enabled FUREE, MOM, and other activists to connect with the broader history of immigrant women's struggles in New York: as the Foundry Theatre notes in promotional copy for the show, the play is "performed by a community that knows what they were singing about in 1937 and what they are singing about in 2011" (the foundrytheatre.org/2011/07/10/pins-needles). The updated version included satire that mocked landlords and figures such as Donald Trump and that criticized the lack of opportunities for New Yorkers in terms of housing, education, and work.

Pins & Needles is different from Ramirez's *Exit Cuckoo*, as it confronts the New York class divide without softening its criticisms of privileged New Yorkers. The roots of the play in the labor movement as well as the experiences of the performers as both exploited New Yorkers and organizers possibly accounts for this difference. Strachan performed in songs such as "Chain Store Daisy," a retelling of the women's low paid labor at Macy's. In a later scene, "Activists Born," Strachan elaborated on her own path from jobs at Macy's and McDonald's to the Work Experience Program that brought her to MOM: "I always feel like I'm not good enough. . . . I just have to work at McDonalds or work at these underpaid jobs just to survive and that's all I really felt I was good enough to do." Joining the cast of *Pins & Needles* provided her with a chance to draw on her theatrical and musical talents and gave her a public venue in which she could critique the narrow work opportunities that had reinforced her sense that she was not deserving or capable of work that could support her and be meaningful at the same time. Strachan expressed gratitude for the opportunity to perform, and her performance was enthusiastically received by MOM and ally groups.

The *New York Times* published a review of *Pins & Needles* that connected the skills activists and performers share: "The big voice and dramatic flair that served [FUREE's] Wanda Imasuen well as a community organizer are turning out to translate nicely to another stage: musical comedy" (Lee, "Cut"). The willingness to be loud and dramatic was important to groups such as MOM and CAAAV. Protest and theater served to bring the challenges experienced by immigrants and women of color into public view. Activists got attention for their campaigns and were able to disrupt the casual acceptance of status quo inequities using these creative strategies. Finally, the ability to assert their position and get a response from those outside their circles sustained their energy during the ups and downs of their campaigns.

In performances, activist-artists seek to carry the passion of protest into theaters, and actors dramatize their own experiences to connect with audiences. Performers in *Exit Cuckoo* and *Pins & Needles* sought to reach multiple audiences from *New York Times* reviewers and off-Broadway theatergoers to low-income community members, workers, and activists (Gates, "Surviving"; Lee "Cut"). Former nanny, playwright, and actress Lisa Ramirez partnered with domestic worker activists to explore dynamics between employers and workers, while MOM organizer Nova Strachan joined Brooklyn's FUREE revival of a union musical to draw attention to economic and housing exploitation in the present day. Both plays provide a unique platform through which to convey the lived consequences of inequality and bring attention to the organizations seeking to challenge its root causes. While neither CAAAV nor MOM has a formalized arts wing or focused on the arts in its mission, they both show an openness to engagement with artistic expression through collaboration.

Though protest and theater helped fuel organizing efforts to raise awareness about specific issues and politicize community members and allies, activists also found it necessary to turn to more liberal means to achieve their aims. As they became more knowledgeable about the issues that concerned them, they began securing basic wins for their communities through the courts. When targets failed to respond to their complaints, both MOM and CAAAV groups used legal strategies to complement their other organizing methods. Outreach and protests helped garner public support for their legal efforts and prevented litigation from overtaking the community-based practices that are at the foundation of their organizations. MOM and CAAAV activists refused to be sidelined by the lack of formal educational experience required of legal advocates. Instead, they worked with experts who could engage with the forms of community knowledge that activists brought to their work. The force of law has proven to be particularly useful when MOM and CAAAV have sought to challenge actors who are distant from the communities that they exploit, rendering them unlikely to respond to more hands-on engagement efforts. The ability of each group to adapt and find means of overcoming this distance has helped them carve out more space for their communities in a time when the global wealth gap is increasing, particularly across racial groups in the United States.

Importantly, in their legal forays, CAAAV and MOM rely heavily on the networks they have created through their organizing efforts and the knowledge of their members rather than solely on outside experts. The cases discussed in the following section highlight why legal strategies matter to the long-term work of both groups. For example, domestic worker Nancy Ventic was able to pursue legal redress as she faced abuses that are all too common in the field, including the withholding of wages, because of her connections to CAAAV through the Filipina domestic worker network whose members included Inday Baldivia and organizer Carolyn De Leon. Similarly, MOM's efforts to shut down polluters in the South Bronx finally bore fruit when it filed a lawsuit, serving to compel the city to begin meeting its demands beyond simply shutting down one factory. The combination of grassroots mobilizations and legal strategies deployed in identity-based social movements of the twentieth century from LGBT activism to the Black civil rights movement continues to be important to activists.

MOM's turn to the law came after New York Organic Fertilizer Company failed to respond to its calls for improvements. In 2008, the National Resource Defense Council, a mainstream environmental advocacy, approached MOM about initiating a lawsuit to protest both the company's continuing pollution and the failure of the city's Department of Environmental Protection to record and address complaints by residents (Warren, "Hunts Point"). There was a growing sense that without the lawsuit, the company would continue to ignore the community's concerns and that the city would continue to refuse to respond to complaints or enforce regulations. The lawsuit was filed against the City of New York, the Department of Environmental Protection, the fertilizer company, its operators (Synagro Technologies), and its corporate investor (the Carlyle Group). In the wake of increasing media attention to MOM's campaign, Congressman José Serrano publicly endorsed it. Andrew Cuomo, the New York State attorney general at the time, followed the National Resource Defense Council suit with his own lawsuit claiming that the site "created a public nuisance under New York State law by producing odors that 'unreasonably interfere with the comfortable enjoyment of life or property" (ag.ny.gov/press-release/attorney-general-cuomo-sues-south-bronx-fertilizer -company-end-noxious-odors-threaten). This case brought enough pressure on the Department of Environmental Protection to compel it to address the concerns of MOM and the South Bronx community. It ordered the fertilizer company to close its doors for a minimum of two years, and the city agreed to stop sending its treated sewage to the plant (Hirsch, "NYOFCo"). Instead of continuing to resist MOM's calls for a study of the causes of poor air quality in the South Bronx, the Department of Environmental Protection also announced an independent odor study of the area's wastewater treatment plant, implemented odor controls, and contributed to the remediation of city-owned land that would become part of the Barretto Point Park (www1.nyc.gov/html /dep/html/press_releases/10-66pr.shtml#.XJKNZFNKiCQ). These concrete actions demonstrated that a significant shift had occurred in the city's approach to community concerns in the South Bronx (Sze, *Noxious New York*, 62). Barbara White, a community elder and longtime member of MOM, noted that the campaign challenged the broader assumption that the South Bronx was an industrial wasteland rather than home to New Yorkers with a voice: "We have made the politicians look at us in the South Bronx in a different light. They have to think twice before they put anything in our neighborhood that we don't want, because they know they will have to face Mothers on the Move" (Mackenzie, "Sweet Smell," 6).

CAAAV has resorted to the law to address individual cases of abuse and has also been a force behind the creation of new legislation. It has a longer history than MOM of appealing to the law when other approaches have failed; for example, it gave testimony in support of the Hate Crimes Sentencing Act of 1992 as part of its push for state action in response to continuing anti-Asian violence. CAAAV's Women Workers Project activists took up the long-standing problem of domestic workers' basic labor rights not being protected under the law. Working as part of Domestic Workers United, they secured major legislative successes: the 2003 passage of Local Law 33 in New York City and the New York State Domestic Workers' Bill of Rights. Local Law 33 requires employment agencies to provide "a written statement indicating the rights of such employee and the obligations of his or her employer under state and federal law," including information about minimum wage, paid overtime, and unemployment insurance, to both potential workers and employers. The New York City law is limited; it does not address working conditions and only applies to domestic workers employed by agencies. The New York State Domestic Workers' Bill of Rights, however, is broader. Under the bill, live-in domestic workers now are to be paid 1.5 times their regular rate after forty-four hours of work instead of 1.5 times the minimum wage, while for live-out domestic workers, the threshold at which overtime kicks in is forty hours, and all workers are entitled to three paid days off after one year of work (knowyourrightsny.org). Finally, the law establishes a review of "the feasibility and practicality of domestic workers organizing for the purpose of collective bargaining" (Domestic Workers United and National Employment Law Project, *Rights*, 18). This review could change the future of organizing efforts by groups such as Domestic Workers United because it could enable these workers to exercise a right on the state level that is specifically prohibited by the federal National Labor Relations Act.

Domestic Workers United's efforts on the city and state level relied on the knowledge and experiences of the Women Workers Project's initial domestic worker membership. Filipina domestic workers in Hong Kong were used to mandatory contract agreements between themselves and their employers. While the Hong Kong contract system is far from perfect when it comes to preventing labor abuses, at least contracts are required, whereas in the United States, as De Leon pointed out, "A lot of people are just getting hired through word of mouth, everything is verbal agreement." Thus, while there is indeed a global problem of employers making their "own rules," Filipinas saw that informal contracts and verbal agreements lacking the legal force of any governmental policies carried more risks for laborers. According to De Leon, "That's when we started investigating.... Women Workers Project had a standard contract that we tailored ... to make it better ... [and] super clear." The idea of a contract thus became part of the Women Workers Project and the Domestic Workers Union organizing work with individual workers and then part of workshops. Finally, it developed into a central component of the organization's efforts to engage employers and set labor standards through Local Law 33 and the Domestic Workers' Bill of Rights.

The Women Workers Project sought not just to change laws but also to support immigrant women's access to the system when they faced exploitation. Member Nancy Ventic's employer attempted to forcibly send her back to the Philippines when he terminated her employment as a live-in domestic worker after she complained about having to work ninety hours a week for two to three dollars an hour. She escaped from her employer's building at the last minute with the help of Women Workers Project members. As Ventic recalled the events of that day, she "had no place to go, don't know where I'm going, but I'm so depressed. But, luckily, ... Inday [another member] give me a call and there is Carolyn who has always open arms to help me" (interview with author, March 21, 2009). Faced with the threat of being forcibly returned to the Philippines, Ventic was understandably anxious and worried. She remembered that "I was afraid that maybe she [Carolyn] really can't help me." However, De Leon and other project activists turned out to be reliable. "Then there she is in a few hours, she's there in the bottom of my building to pick me up with some of her friends in the cab. So Carol take me through her place and she introduced me about CAAAV that they can really help me and my situation." After it became clear to Ventic that CAAAV's Women Workers Project activists were indeed there for her, she began to see herself as part of the group.

Ventic received support from the group to bring a lawsuit against her former employer for back pay that was covered by the local news in 2004 (Casimir and Shin, "Group Urges"). While initially unsure about CAAAV, she became a participant and saw her experience as positive: "From time to time I attend the meeting; I learned a lot; it opened my mind and my heart that there's a certain person that really help and a certain organization can help my case." Not only did she get assistance, but she began to be more knowledgeable about her rights and came to understand that her experience was part of a larger pattern of abuse against domestic workers. Ventic was surprised that her case moved forward and was successful: "Then in a few months, within a year, my case was resolved.... Thank God to the help of CAAAV, it's a big victory, my case" (interview with author, March 21, 2009). Working with CAAAV's Women Workers Project enabled Ventic not only to escape an abusive employment situation but also to get paid for her work. With her own struggle largely won, Ventic continued to maintain a relationship with the group, De Leon, and Baldivia, suggesting the potential for long-term ties to develop out of such crises.

The use of legal approaches by both MOM and CAAAV suggests that grassroots groups can utilize professional services without undercutting the agency and expertise of their members. In both cases, it was critical that the laws or lawsuits were not seen as the final goal of campaigns: "An issue that can be won only through a lawsuit," as the Midwest Academy observes, "is not the kind that builds leadership, as the key decision-making and negotiation roles tend to be limited to lawyers and judges" (Sen, *Stir It Up*, 51). These legal pursuits were one component in a long-term struggle to improve the conditions of the South Bronx and domestic workers, reflecting a holistic approach that recognizes the limitations of legal solutions to problems that are complex and deeply woven into the social, political, and economic fabric of a given area.

This chapter's review of key organizing approaches by MOM and CAAAV demonstrates both the complexity of the issues they addressed and their flexibility in approaching these issues over the 1990s and 2000s. The recent and long histories of the groups are tied together. Domestic workers from the Philippines acknowledged that the history of African enslavement and the experience of Black women were important to their movement through their organizing practices and more public acts like a stop during a march at lower Manhattan's African Burial Ground National Monument. CAAAV and MOM activists traveled across the city to come together and support tenants' rights in Manhattan's Chinatown and El Barrio neighborhoods. Their work reflects Elsa Barkley Brown's insight that history is indeed "everybody talking at once, multiple rhythms being played simultaneously. The events and people we write about did not occur in isolation but in dialogue with a myriad of other people and events" ("'What Has Happened,'" 295–312). MOM and CAAAV activists are part of global struggles for racial, gender, environmental, and economic justice. Without an approach that embraces cacophony, it is not possible to acknowledge points of harmony in organizing and message, the dominant rhythms of late capitalism, and the atonality of complex individuals' lives and communities. Their reliance on mixed methods demonstrates their commitment to using whatever means are available to address issues that are at the heart of their queer motherwork praxis. They refused to overvalue political purity, such as ignoring legal strategies on account of their leftist critique of the state, or a singular organizing model, such as only engaging with public housing residents and not a broader world of allies. The next chapter considers how both groups have taken on housing organizing as part of their effort to fight for a future for their communities.

CHAPTER 4

Housing Struggles from Chinatown to the South Bronx

> The right to the city is far more than the individual liberty to access urban resources: it is a right to change ourselves by changing the city.... [T]his transformation inevitably depends upon the exercise of a collective power to reshape the processes of urbanization. The freedom to make and remake our cities and ourselves is ... one of the most precious yet most neglected of our human rights.
>
> **DAVID HARVEY, "THE RIGHT TO THE CITY"**

> This is a home. Why should money make me move?
>
> **ZHI QI ZHENG, QUOTED IN MICHAEL POWELL,**
> **"HER CHINATOWN IS UNDERPERFORMING"**

Defending Home

CAAAV housing organizer Zhi Qi Zheng who, along with her neighbors, had been harassed and neglected by an investment firm that had recently purchased her Manhattan Chinatown tenement building at 61 Delancey Street rhetorically asked a *New York Times* reporter why she should accept a buyout offer for her apartment. The struggle over affordable housing in New York plays a large part in the histories of MOM and CAAAV. This issue was of particular concern in the new millennium, as New York City housing prices accelerated despite the fluctuating economy in the 2000s. As part of a citywide coalition called New York is Our Home!, in May 2007, MOM activists traveled by bus from the Bronx to Manhattan to raise their voices as tenants about the growing problem. The coalition demanded affordable protections for section 8 housing and called for limiting rent increases for vulnerable residents, including the elderly and those living with HIV/AIDS. As MOM's Paulette New explained to reporters, "I don't want to say it's always about money, but it's always about the money.... The landlords keep the tenants uninformed, and then they take advantage of the tenants who don't know their rights" (Ahmed, "Hunts Point").

Community members and activists such as New and Zheng brought their own experiences as residents struggling to keep their homes to an activism grounded in their concern for others in a similar situation. MOM and CAAAV provided a platform for community members to respond to rising inequalities. They also offered them a deeper understanding of both the drivers of inequity and outlined the options for demanding justice for low-income New Yorkers in the city. Housing formed a core component of both groups' queer motherwork approach.

Organized housing struggles have long been a part of New York history. Immigrants and poor residents have been fighting for places to live since the turn of the twentieth century. For groups such as CAAAV and MOM, the movement for affordable housing became a key part of their organizational work. As housing costs increased and real estate development of the city seeking to attract affluent residents from across the globe exploded, these activists joined with allies fighting similar battles across the United States and the globe. Both CAAAV and MOM treat housing as a basic need and as a human right and approach it through an intersectional lens that recognizes role of gender, in combination with class, race, and nation, in the struggles of residents and their efforts to guarantee a future for themselves, their families, and their communities in New York.

As a New York resident living in poorly maintained private housing on the border of Harlem and Washington Heights for the majority of my ethnographic research, I saw the same housing violations in many buildings and witnessed the targeting of immigrant-of-color residents by management companies and landlords. The management company for our building had lied to my Spanish–speaking Dominican and Puerto Rican neighbors about not receiving their rent and had threatened them with eviction; they were viewed as vulnerable based on their language abilities and possible immigration status and as not valuable as low-income renters. Basic repairs were not completed, and our supers were fired if they began to carry out needed repairs. However, while my neighborhood began losing local businesses due to increasing rents and the northward encroachment of Columbia University, there was a time lag before the escalating rents in Chinatown, Harlem, and, increasingly, Washington Heights transformed into higher income and whiter neighborhoods. But eventually, gentrification became a problem up and down Manhattan, making broad-based organizing to address issues across neighborhoods as well as within buildings critical.

Residents whose lives were often forgotten in narratives of New York City's reemergence as the world's most competitive global city in the 1990s (Karni, "NYC Crowned") came together through groups like MOM and CAAAV to protest the injustices they experienced, demanding that individual, corporate, or government landlords respect their basic rights and allow them to continue to live in their communities. The conflicts created by the ascendance of global capital enterprises and the concentration of marginalized populations in a global city raises the question, as sociologist Saskia Sassen notes, of "Whose city is it?" ("Global City," 39). In the 2000s, corporate entities bought up residential buildings and began courting the wealthiest residents. In 2013, the top fifth of New Yorkers had a mean income of $222,871, and the top 5% had a mean income of $436,931 (Roberts, "Poverty Rate"). At the same time, the income gap had widened, with the city's poverty rate increasing to 21.2% in 2012 (in contrast to the oft-critiqued federal poverty threshold level, owing to the basic cost of living, is generally considered by progressives to be set too low) with a mean of $8,993 for the lowest fifth of New Yorkers (www.ssc.wisc.edu/irpweb/faqs/faq2.htm). The response of the left to this chasm was to argue that housing is a human right, an idea articulated most directly by the Right to the City Alliance that MOM and CAAAV joined. CAAAV's and MOM's identity- and community-based organizing demonstrated that the answer to the question of whose home New York was was thus a loud, defiant "Ours!" Their mobilizations to defend low-income immigrant and residents of color are key examples of queer motherwork and the identity-based politics that are at the heart of this book; MOM and CAAAV named and responded to the complex and often hidden interests and practices that undercut access to affordable and safe housing.

Gendering Housing History

For over a century, women have been crucial participants in New York City's tenants' rights activism; their long-standing engagement reflects the fact that housing is "both a universal need and, ironically, an entity located in the 'domestic sphere' of conventional gender ideology" (Gold, "'I Had Not,'" 388). Women built and maintained the movement that emerged out of early rent strikes at the turn of the twentieth century (Lawson and Barton, "Sex Roles"). They began taking on formal leadership roles in neighborhood organizations by the 1920s (Lawson and Barton, "Sex Roles," 233). In the late 1950s, in the wake of the economic boom jumpstarted by World War II, women organized against urban renewal plans that threatened their neighborhoods (Gold, "'I Had Not'"; 390; Carroll, *Mobilizing*). While poor and working-class women of all backgrounds sought to defend and improve housing, during the same period of the late 1950s and 1960s, there was a "woman's fight" to open up public housing to low-income New Yorkers of color (Jackson, "Harlem's Rent Strike," 61). As noted by historian Roberta Gold, in these multiracial tenant mobilizations in the 1960s and 1970s "women's authority was not only tolerated but seen as normal" ("'I Had Not,'" 399).

Poverty, an overlapping concern, is likewise both a universal and gendered concern because women make up a large proportion of the world's poor, and women-led households are and have been disproportionately poor (World Bank, "Inside"). During the period that the research for this book was conducted from the mid-2000s into the early 2010s, the Bronx led New York's boroughs with the highest rate of overall poverty, and almost one-half of women-led households in the Bronx were living in poverty. Public housing offered affordable housing, particularly for women-led households. Battles over New York public housing date back to the 1950s, when women participated in fights against evictions of people of color from the New York City Housing Authority (NYCHA) buildings. NYCHA's housing policies became increasingly discriminatory, and it withheld adequate sanitation services in a manner that dehumanized residents. American Studies scholar Mandi Isaacs Jackson argues that the challenges faced by New Yorkers in the 1950s and 1960s have not gone away in the twenty-first century, as "affordable housing remains scarce, wages remain unequal, and the walls erected by racism in the nation's largest northern metropolis remain intact" ("Harlem's Rent Strike," 74). Her claim that affordable housing is hard to come by is supported by the fact that in 2013, the number of individuals and families on the waiting list for homes eclipsed the number of public housing apartments in the NYCHA system (Navarro, "227,000 Names"). This gap increased with the rising costs of housing in New York City, further lengthening the seemingly endless wait for NYCHA apartments. Women-led households make up a disproportionate number of public housing households. According to NYCHA's 2015 reporting, the system housed 131,364 families with a female head of household, compared to 30,797 families with a male head of household, a gap that is consistently reflected in NYCHA's residential data from the 1960s onward (www1.nyc.gov/assets/nycha/downloads/pdf/res_data.pdf). Through their work with NYCHA residents, MOM and CAAAV address the intersecting gender and class issue of affordable housing in New York.

CAAAV built its public housing outreach in the 2010s, seeking to support Asians, particularly those with limited English proficiency, who were living in public housing. For groups such as MOM and CAAAV, working to ensure that public housing continued to be an option for their communities and that it improved in quality was an extension of their existing queer motherwork praxis that addressed the needs of poor and low-income New Yorkers.

CAAAV made the connection between housing and women's outsized role in housing at a 2011 Mother's Day march in Manhattan's Chinatown. As part of CAAAV's team, I attended this rally and helped provide security support to ensure marchers' safety as they crossed the area's busy streets. CAAAV members and allies, along with English and Chinese press, met at Sara Roosevelt Park for a rally to support tenants' rights and stronger rent laws. Roosevelt Park is a long thin city park that runs between the bustling Chrystie and Forsyth Streets from Chinatown through the Lower East Side. CAAAV organizer Zhi Qi Zheng was a notable presence as usual, greeting Chinatown residents and allies alike as they congregated before the march kicked off. Zheng had immigrated to the United States thirty years before and raised her four children in Chinatown, laboring in a Chinatown garment factory until it, along with half of the area's factories, closed in the wake of the September 11, 2001 attacks (Tsui, "City"). After a relative began struggling with housing issues, Zheng joined CAAAV and became a housing organizer who would both advocate for tenant rights and fight for her own home in Chinatown. The group that assembled for the Mother's Day march was largely composed of Chinatown Tenants Union and Chinatown Justice Project members. We walked across the neighborhood, stopping at 11 Allen Street, 54 Eldridge Street, and 55 Delancey Street to draw attention to the ongoing campaigns to support those building's residents as they fought back against landlord neglect and harassment (Jiang, "Dozens"). As CAAAV housing organizer Esther Wang told reporters: "Pretty much every day we have someone coming to us with a new story of a landlord harassing them" (Barbarino, "Chinese Residents"). Through the Mother's Day march, CAAAV underscored women's long-standing commitment to housing organizing in New York City and its embrace of motherwork. MOM and CAAAV activists used such strategies to counter the status quo faced by low-income residents and increasing threats to their ability to reside in New York.

Chinatown as Home

As of 2010, Chinese New Yorkers composed 47% of the city's Asian community (Asian American Federation, "2010 Census Data"). New York's overall Asian population rapidly grew over the decade, making up 12.6% of New Yorkers and topping one million for the first time (New York City Department of Planning, *NYC2010*). The neighborhoods with the largest Chinese representation were Brooklyn's Sunset Park East and Bensonhurst West; Flushing, Queens; and Manhattan's Chinatown. The city's oldest Chinatown is located within the bounds of Manhattan's historically working-class, immigrant Lower East Side. As journalist Bonnie Tsui observed in 2009, "The New York neighborhood's biggest battle now is over gentrification and the displacement of its working class" ("City," 74). Drawing on U.S. census data, the Asian American Federation reported that the neighborhood had lost 17% of its Chinese residents between 2000 and 2010 ("2010 Census Data"). New York City comptroller Scott Stringer's office released data that showed a 13% decline in the number of Asian residents in Chinatown and the Lower East Side between 2000 and 2015 (Small, "Gentrification"). As shown in figure 5, the newer outer borough Chinatowns of Sunset Park East, Brooklyn, and Flushing, Queens, expanded, coming to outnumber the Manhattan neighborhood's Chinese population (Small, "Gentrification"; Asian American Federation, "2010 Census Data"; Beekman, "Changing Chinatowns"; Khan, "Making Census").

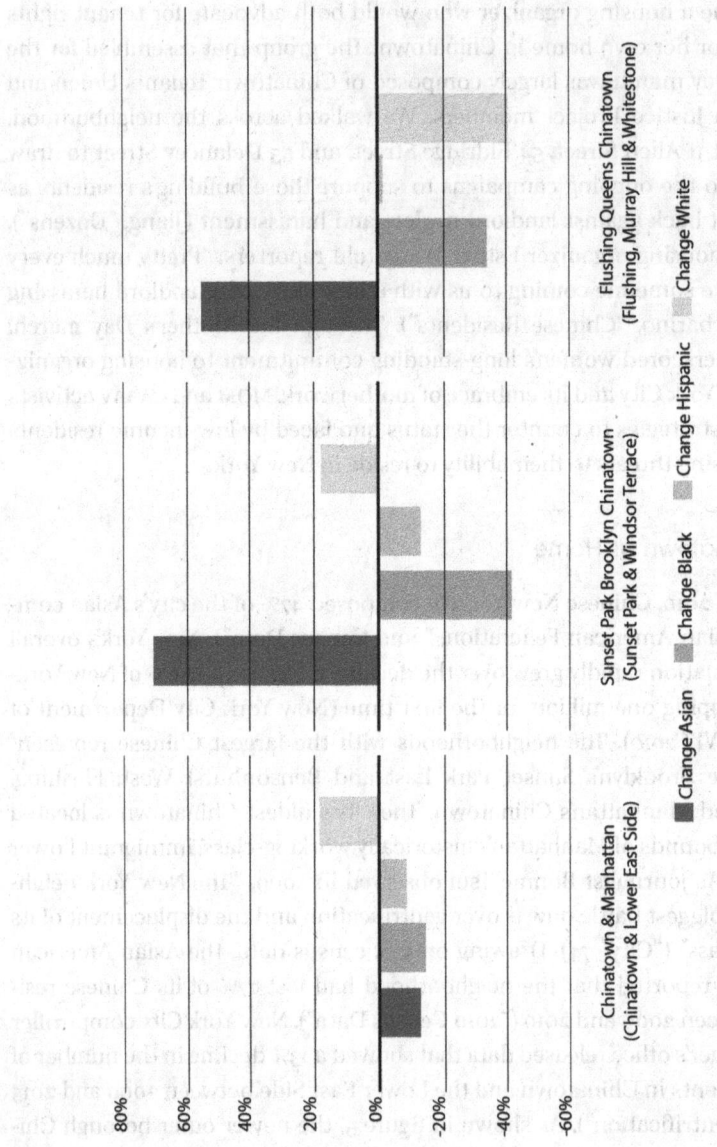

FIGURE 5. Chinatown demographic shifts, 2000–2015. CityLab 2018.

Throughout the decade, CAAAV worked in Manhattan Chinatown to defend tenants' rights as residents faced increasing pressure from landlords, developers, and at times, city agencies, to leave their neighborhood. As housing organizer Zhi Qi Zheng observed, "The changes are incredible—rents are going up all the time and landlords are trying to evict us whatever way they can" (CAAAV, "Right," 8). Zheng's tireless efforts with CAAAV volunteer Bin Liang on behalf of tenants' rights during this period earned them the "dynamic duo" moniker within their group (CAAAV, "Right," 10). Liang brought her thirty years of teaching experience in China to their door-to-door outreach to tenants, during which she and Zheng spoke with tenants about their rights and invited them to participate in the work of the Chinatown Tenants Union. CAAAV celebrated the team's commitment in CAAAV's newsletter: "In any given week, they will climb an average of 50 stories, knock on over 150 doors, and talk to over 100 people about the Chinatown Tenants Union in Fujianese, Cantonese, AND Mandarin" (CAAAV, "Right," 10). Zheng and Liang collaborated with CAAAV housing organizers and volunteers to build the Chinatown Tenants Union that by 2007 had a base of over thirteen hundred supporters. Zheng emphasized how crucial coalitions are in seeking change, noting that "it's really important to be part of a movement because by ourselves, our voices are really small; . . . we need to let our targets know that we are not just by ourselves, that we actually have a voice and we have power" (dailymotion.com/video/x2s5pe1). The group's Chinatown Justice Project in conjunction with the Chinatown Tenants Union helped organizers develop a strong voice in the area, and CAAAV's office at 191 East 3rd Street was close to the neighborhood. The Chinatown Justice Project ran a twelve-month-long program intended to train and raise the consciousness of Chinese youth. This program helped CAAAV intensify its organizing efforts in the community and train a younger generation of activists who would become future leaders, including Helena Wong, who was executive director during the late 2000s, and ManSee Kong, a filmmaker-activist (Bobadilla, "Feministing Five").

The history of these efforts make evident CAAAV's refusal to let low-income residents be run out of their homes. On July 27, 2000, the justice project members held a press conference announcing the release of its report on housing and environmental conditions in Manhattan's Chinatown (a copy of which can be found in the CAAAV papers). The report, which was based on surveys of one hundred residents conducted by Chinatown Justice Project members, noted that 50% were paying $600 to $1000 a month in rent while the median annual family income in the Chinatown/Lower East Side area was $17,100, which meant that 40% to 70% of those household incomes were being used to pay rent. More than a third of those surveyed reported living in one- to two-bedroom apartments with households of six or more people, 58% reported lacking hot water, 42% had plumbing problems, and 37% did not have adequate heat in their apartments. Youth organizer JingJing Lin stated: "Many people blame new immigrants as the cause of Chinatown's housing problems, especially overcrowding, but our research shows otherwise." Activists argued that area's high rent to low wage ratio was the primary cause of apartment overcrowding, not that there were too many people trying to living in Chinatown. In addition to the high costs of rent and lack of proper building maintenance, residents reported being forced to pay up to $6,000 in "key money," an upfront cash payment that was illegal and off the books, to receive keys to a rental unit in addition to rent and security deposits. A total of 43% of survey respondents had paid key money to secure their current apartments. Paying key money enabled them to secure housing but did not guarantee their long-term ability to stay in the neighborhood.

The report found that government subsidies for the construction of luxury condominiums on Orchard and Ludlow Streets had resulted in a drastic demographic shift, as the area went from being majority Chinese immigrant to increasingly high-income white. CAAAV's youth member Sauling Chan explained that life in the area was becoming increasingly hostile, with race and class dictating how tenants were treated by their landlords.

> There are buildings on Mott and Mulberry owned by the same landlord, but they're very, very different.... On Mulberry, where there are mostly white tenants, the building is nice and tenants say they don't [have] much problem with their landlord. But on Mott Street, I was surprised to see the building is so bad. The stairs are broken, there's holes in the ceilings and floors, it's dirty and dark in the hallways. We say the landlord has a different face for a different race. (Lobbia, "Civics Lesson")

Fenzhen Nie, another youth member, added, "The point is not the race of the landlord but the tenant.... Even a Chinese landlord wants to gentrify and bring in white people who make more money. They treat tenants differently based on race." Elizabeth Dwoskin's 2010 *Village Voice* article "When Hipsters Move in on Chinese: It's Ugly" highlights these tensions. Her piece recounts the experience of an art student, Anna Bakker, who moved into a three-bedroom apartment at 55 Delancey Street, one of the buildings owned by Madison Capital, a real estate investment and operating company that at the time held over $2.5 billion in assets. CAAAV had been battling Madison Capital over its efforts to displace Chinese tenants in the neighborhood. Madison Capital's website described the 55 Delancey Street property as an "underperforming 6-story, walk up building in the heart of the Lower East Side." Upon the acquisition of the building in April 2008, "Madison commenced a repositioning strategy which included the re-leasing of vacant rental units and the renovation and re-leasing of under market residential apartments"—in other words, the company undertook to improve apartments and then rent them to new,

IMAGE 4. Chinatown community struggle exhibition, August 24, 2008.
Photo by Ariella Rotramel.

higher-paying residents instead of the existing tenants. Bakker and her friends were the targets of these efforts, and they happily moved into the apartment when it had been "extensively renovated, with clean floors, a new fridge, and a fresh coat of paint." The article addresses the ongoing struggles of long-term tenants to fight harassment from the building's owners and the different way these residents were treated from the new arrivals. The new renters showed little interest in the plight of the long-term residents. Dwoskin's article concludes with a statement from graphic designer Hannah Lavon: "'I'm sorry it's [gentrification] happening, but—' she pauses, then shrugs—'I like the apartment.'" This remark underscored the importance of the Chinatown Justice Project's report and ongoing efforts to support tenants' rights as they encountered wealthier landlords and renters who would displace them from their homes with no more than a shrug.

On August 24, 2008, the Chinatown Justice Project and Chinatown Tenants Union organized an exhibition entitled "Chinatown Community Struggle." That warm Sunday, youth members in their bright green union T-shirts welcomed passing Chinatown residents as they strolled through Sara Roosevelt Park, where rows of T-shirts hung across a playing field. I attended the event and was struck by the enthusiasm and positive energy that the youth brought to discussing such a troubling issue.

The text and images on the T-shirts documented key moments in the history of gentrification in Chinatown since the 1970s as well as issues like the mass evictions of Chinatown residents, the rise of condo developments, and the proposed privatization of public housing throughout the city. One T-shirt from the Chinatown exhibit summarized the union's work: "Through organizing residents, direct action campaigns, and working in alliance with other organizations, CTU's mission is to protect low-income tenants in Chinatown from gentrification and displacement."

Founded in 2005, the Chinatown Tenants Union had a broad organizing base of residents ranging from high school youth to mature and elderly residents. Through the union, CAAAV worked "to ensure that residents play a key role in community-led development and that those processes are democratic, equitable, and just." The union sought to build "the power of low-income tenants by developing their leadership and engaging in strategic organizing campaigns." According to a now defunct web page outlining the project, these campaigns included "working with individual tenants or all tenants in one building to address housing issues," "waging campaigns that expand tenants' rights, change City policy, and protect Chinatown from gentrification and overdevelopment," and "participating in the broader movement to fight for housing, immigrant, and economic justice." This approach enabled CAAAV to address immediate crises faced by Chinatown tenants as they face eviction or harassment by landlords while developing residents' knowledge of the broader context of developments that have increased pressure on residents and that may be countered by mass social justice movements.

Another T-shirt narrated the transformation of the triangle at Canal, Baxter, and Walker Streets from a center for local Chinatown fruit and vegetable vendors into an information kiosk for tourists (Rotramel, "We Make the Spring Rolls"). Former New York City Mayor Rudolph Giuliani launched the plan to move the vendors out with his Quality of Life campaign. The T-shirt described how "cops kicked vendors out of the triangle" and from neighborhoods across the city. This aggressive approach to policing contributed to a perceived targeting of people of color that most famously drew protests with the 1999 police shooting death of Amadou Diallo (Rand, *Ellis Island*, 204). Mayor Bloomberg's administration supported a final effort to gain control over the space and in 2004 constructed a kiosk in the triangle as part of the Explore Chinatown campaign, an initiative funded by the Lower Manhattan Development Corporation and the September 11th Fund with support from the New York City Department of Transportation and Department of Parks (www.renewnyc.com/Newsletters/March2005/). The exhibit's shirts spoke to issues that predated Chinatown's emergence as a "last frontier" for development, demonstrating the knowledge that youth members gained through their work with CAAAV

IMAGE 5. Evicted T-shirt, August 24, 2008. Photo by Ariella Rotramel.

PLEASE JOIN US CHINATOWN TENANT UNION TO PREVENT MORE EVICTIONS

驱赶

请加入我们的唐人街住客协会来防止驱赶！现在！

(Zimmer, "Chinatown"; La Ferla, "General Tso's"; Grieve, "The *Times*"; Hope, "Changes Afoot"; Smith, "New City," CAAAV and Urban Justice Center 2008). They also communicated the high costs of gentrification and displacement and the attendant need for action, most intensely in an "Evicted" T-shirt that called for residents to unite in the struggle against evictions.

Reclaiming Public Housing's Promise

In the 2000s, MOM activists joined CAAAV in several of their protests in Chinatown to support residents fighting for improved living conditions and against evictions. They recognized a connection between the issues tenants faced in Chinatown and the challenges public and private housing residents faced in the South Bronx. Its early work included building support for rent strikes in buildings run by the Banana Kelly Community Improvement Association, a dysfunctional nonprofit organization. In the early 2000s, its efforts resulted in an investigation by the state's attorney general and prompted both a replacement of the group's board and improved services for residents (Grossman, "Banana Kelly"; Office of the Attorney General New York, "Spitzer"). This approach reflected MOM's focus on housing activism that challenged the isolation that residents commonly felt despite their sharing the experience of their needs being ignored. As MOM member Joyce Culler stated at the 2007 "New York Is Our Home" rally, "The next step is to get the attention of and talk to our local politicians. We're just getting started" (Ahmed, "Hunts Point"). MOM's work persuaded residents that their demands could be heard and that they had the ability to hold their representatives accountable.

Nova Strachan, MOM housing organizer, sought to build residents' power in the city's embattled public housing through this strategic approach. Strachan was born and raised by her grandmother in the NYCHA's Claremont Consolidated Houses (interview with author, March 5, 2008). The Claremont Consolidated Houses made the news in the summer of 2012 when residents reported a rat infestation problem that had been ignored by NYCHA officials until it became public knowledge (CBS News New York, "Bronx Public Housing"). When working with NYCHA residents, Strachan would emphasize that "if we don't band together now, then it's going to be too late when you realize, 'Oh, I should've gone to this meeting, I should've talked to this person, or I should've done this that and the third.'" It was fundamental that residents get the information they needed and respond to injustice before they found themselves at the mercy of governmental officials and development interests seeking to shrink public housing.

Early in her role as MOM's lead housing organizer, Strachan facilitated the creation of the group's Tenants Rallying in Unity to Maintain Public Housing, beginning in the St. Mary's Park houses in the late 2000s. Like CAAAV's Chinatown Tenants Union, the group emphasized the importance of developing leadership among residents and addressing the range of housing issues they encountered. Strachan described the importance of building unity among residents:

> Without that trust between the tenants, knowing that we're all in this together, it really doesn't go nowhere. . . . [The group is] something to show the other [public housing] residents that we're trying to pull into our organization that, "Look, these tenants are trying to make a difference, they even came up with a name that emphasizes what we're out here for." We're trying to maintain public housing and at the same time, we have to build unity and do this together.

As an organizer, she recognized that tenants had to establish themselves as neighbors who could be counted on to keep up the fight for well-maintained and affordable public housing.

The need to build a response to the NYCHA was underscored for Strachan when she attended the 2007 U.S. Social Forum in Atlanta, Georgia. She recalled on meeting New Orleans activists after Hurricane Katrina that "I'm thinking, like, what I really need to do, if I can, is stress to these tenants, look at what they're doing to these people in New Orleans. . . . Look how they're bulldozing these people's apartments knowing that there was no damage really done to these apartments, knowing that people's stuff was still in these residences, and we just think nothing can happen to us." From her interactions with housing activists Strachan learned about the ongoing displacement of poor and working-class Blacks in post-Katrina New Orleans, as affordable housing failed to keep pace with the number of lost homes that needed to be replaced, and the reenvisioned city failed to support the return of one hundred thousand Black former residents (Moore, "Stranded Again"; Finger, "Public Housing"; Green, Kouassi, and Mambo, "Housing"). This reality contradicted the assumptions that NYCHA residents made about the commitment of the agency to their housing. As Strachan summarized, residents thought that if the NYCHA was going to remove them from one public housing unit, then it would guarantee comparable housing in another:

> "Oh, if they're gonna privatize the building, they have to find somewhere else for us to live. Oh they can't do that." This is what I hear and this is what almost made me starting believing that, "Yeah they can't do nothing like that to us, we've been here all this time and we pay rent just like everybody else and no [they won't close NYCHA buildings]." Eventually, that's gonna happen to us if we don't do something now.

As the city continued to struggle to maintain public housing buildings while opening up property to private interests, it became increasingly important for tenants to organize to resist their diminishing quality of life and the decrease in available units for them to live in.

At the 2007 U.S. Social Forum, Strachan met "people from all over the world" who "came for the same cause and had so much information and so much strength, and they had their strategies to try to counteract this gentrification that's going on all over the world." Being able to see her place in a broad-based movement helped sustain Strachan in her day-to-day work with NYCHA residents to address the issues they faced daily in their homes. Visiting local NYCHA buildings, she invited tenants to Tenants Rallying in Unity to Maintain Public Housing meetings and MOM events, as well as their building's tenant association meetings. Door knocking is a challenging tactic; from my observations of both groups' work, many residents do not answer their doors or open them only briefly to take fliers,. But Strachan usually managed to have extended conversations about current conditions in the building with at least a few residents on each floor of a building.

While Strachan and I were door knocking in the South Bronx's NYCHA buildings one evening in the spring of 2009, a young woman, who was in the midst of her college finals and lived with her daughter, invited us into her home. Her interior hallway wall had large chunks of peeling paint and her kitchen was in disrepair. These problems were caused by years of little to no maintenance in NYCHA buildings and were similar to the problems the tenants the CAAAV's Chinatown Tenants Union were trying to organize faced in the privately owned, low-income buildings in Chinatown. All our visits to NYCHA housing confirmed a lack of maintenance, including a fall 2010 visit I made with Strachan and two volunteers to NYCHA's Betances complex in Mott Haven housing, where there were rusted, cracked steps in the stairwells and peeling paint in hallways. The failure to carry out repairs could prove deadly, as documented by the *New York Times* in 2008 after the death of a five-year-old boy in Brooklyn as he tried to escape from a stuck elevator. The accompanying audio slide show focused on broken or malfunctioning elevators in NYCHA buildings and includes interviews with frustrated residents (Mainland, Fernandez, and Hansen, "Failed Elevators"). While the NYCHA repeatedly cited safety concerns as its reason for removing residents from their homes at 81 Bowery, it did not display much interest in the housing violations in NYCHA buildings. Rallying around such issues was key to MOM's successes in the 2000s, when it organized in the St. Mary's, E. R. Moore, and Bronxchester houses to address issues such as lack of trash pickup and elevator maintenance (MOM and Urban Justice Center, *Change*). When NYCHA building managers proved unresponsive, MOM organized residents to protest and drew on its relationship with local politicians to push for the replacement of ineffective managers. These efforts led to real improvements within specific buildings but also illustrated ongoing frustrations residents experienced living in public housing buildings and the great lengths they had to go to maintain a livable environment.

As part of its housing justice efforts, MOM also took to the streets. In a 2010 report by MOM's organizing ally Community Voices Heard, the organization argued that "there continues to be a lack of support for positive and functioning resident associations, and even in the best cases, residents have no actual decision-making power over the policies that affect them" (Villano and Youdelman, *Democracy (In)action*, 19; Chen, "Democracy"). Within New York's public housing, there was low association participation (17%) and a lack of awareness of the existence of such groups (47%) (Villano and Youdelman, *Democracy (In)action*, 19). Similar to the leadership in Chicago's Wentworth Gardens and replicating the broader gendered history of housing activism, resident association leaders tended to be older Black women, while levels of participation among youth, men, and Latinxs were low (Villano and Youdelman, *Democracy (In)action*, 13–14). MOM worked consistently to raise awareness about resident associations in buildings, provide materials in Spanish as well as English, and engage youth in housing activism through their Youth on the Move group. Yet there were limits on resident participation stipulated by federal and local policies: "Residents can participate by voicing their concerns on policy, but they cannot actually create and shape policy" (Villano and Youdelman, *Democracy (In)action*, 53). Thus, activists sought out other avenues through which to organize residents and resolve problems.

For example, MOM's participation in a union-led rally for public housing on May 1, 2008, was an opportunity to stand alongside NYCHA workers and place political pressure on the city and federal governments to properly fund public housing. NYCHA workers spoke out about how cuts in funding meant the agency had less janitorial and pest control supplies that it could make available to the bare-bones staff (Union Review, "On May 1"; Santiago, "New York City Tenants"). MOM and Tenants Rallying in Unity to Maintain Public Housing member Ray Smith stated, "I've had neighbors that needed their toilets, doors, stove, Frigidaire fixed and had to wait a long time. . . . And the elevators are broken almost every day. They'll fix it, but it's just temporary" (Santiago, "New York City Tenants"). MOM's queer motherwork efforts sought to ensure the safety, health, and well-being of residents.

In 2010, MOM (as part of the New York City Alliance to Preserve Public Housing) once again made a push to defend public housing. The alliance brought together local organizations and supportive politicians at a June 30 NYCHA public hearing at which organizers requested that concerns ranging from the uprooting of residents to timely repairs be more adequately addressed in the current plan. As the New York City Alliance stated in a press release, "Expedient decisions in the past have resulted in a form of benign neglect. . . . The current deficit continues this unfortunate trend towards surgical solutions that diminish both the number of units available . . . as well as the quality of life for residents" (Culvert Chronicles, "NYC Alliance"). NYCHA's underfunding was not only troubling for residents but it meant fewer jobs—a critical issue for residents of the South Bronx.

MOM also pushed for NYCHA job creation as pockets of money became available. When I accompanied Nova Strachan to the Betances complex, we handed out fliers for an October 14, 2010, meeting with NYCHA environmental coordinator Margarita Lopez to discuss NYCHA's plan to green public housing (email to author, September 27, 2010). There was interest in this program as it would provide residents with a chance to hear directly from Lopez and Michelle Pinnock, NYCHA's senior advisor for resident economic empowerment and sustainability. Held in the community center around the corner from their building, the meeting attracted fifty-five residents who learned about NYCHA's overall plan to update buildings with energy-efficient light bulbs and boilers and to undertake other measures. Officials also discussed the section 3 resident employment program and resident training academy (MOM, "Report"). While there was relatively little stable funding for these programs, these face-to-face encounters showed that there would be community interest in such programs if they could be funded, and these encounters also put pressure on New York officials to fight for better funding of NYCHA projects.

The need for consistent advocacy work was also made apparent to NYCHA after officials failed to "live up to a 2001 commitment to spend 15 percent of the agency's labor costs putting tenants to work on renovation and construction projects in the buildings they live in" (White, "NYCHA Owes Tenants"). In April 2011, MOM members took to the streets of the South Bronx neighborhood of Mott Haven to protest this broken promise. It appeared that Lopez, despite participating in the fall event, had changed her tune. "We're not an employment agency," she told Strachan (White, "NYCHA Owes Tenants"). MOM's promotion of green jobs in NYCHA buildings was a response to the joblessness that residents have regularly faced in the South Bronx. As of February 2011, unemployment in the Bronx was at 12.7%, "more than three percent higher than the national average, and over five percent higher than Manhattan's, according to the U.S. Bureau of Labor" (White, "NYCHA Owes Tenants"). Fortunately, with the rebounding economy and increasing social support, service, and health care jobs, unemployment declined to 6.2% in 2017, though it continued to be higher than the citywide unemployment rate of 4.5% (osc.state.ny.us/osdc /rpt4-2019.pdf).

In the 2010s, MOM and its allies continued to pursue a multipronged approach to fighting for NYCHA residents. In 2013, the agency was reported to have failed to spend $700 million that had been directly allocated for building renovations according to the city's controller, John Liu (Smith, "NYCHA Tenants"). At the same time, the NYCHA had moved forward with plans to lease NYCHA land to developers who wanted to build luxury condos (Smith, "NYCHA Tenants"). This step was concerning for many advocates because it suggested that the city was moving toward privatizing public housing. Activists continued to protest against both the NYCHA's failure to use allocated funds to improve buildings and its opening up of public land to private developers. The highly publicized *Floyd, et al. v. City of New York, et al.* federal class action lawsuit that charged that the New York Police Department's usage of "stop and frisk" was a form of racial profiling was also relevant to NYCHA residents (Center for Constitutional Rights, "Floyd"). The NYPD had frequently arrested NYCHA residents and visitors for trespassing, resulting in the 2010 *Davis v. NYCHA and City of New York* lawsuit that argued that racial profiling was driving up rates of arrests of people of color and threatening their constitutional right to access public housing. "We are tired of being humiliated by police," Strachan said. "I'm tired of being harassed by cops in my own building, and avoiding inviting family and friends over for fear of them being arrested just by paying me a visit" (NAACP Legal Defense and Educational Fund, "Stop and Frisks"). Akai Gurley's shooting death that CAAAV activists' organized around was the direct result of policing in public housing, demonstrating how such practices could, in fact, endanger residents.

Overlapping Issues in Housing and Community Spaces

In the 2010s, identity came to the foreground, as MOM and CAAAV activists organized around issues relating to waterfront usage and police violence and responded to the aftermath of Hurricane Sandy. Both groups had long been advocating for more inclusive public spaces in their areas so that low-income residents could comfortably participate in activities such as walking and play. MOM helped push for the creation of Barretto Point Park that looks out onto the East River in the industrialized neighborhood of Hunts Point. Moreover, MOM was able, as part of the Southern Bronx River Watershed Alliance (founded in 1999) with other local groups, to move forward with a longtime plan to reimagine the Sheridan Expressway. The Robert Moses–era highway cuts through the South Bronx; it was built to support commercial truck traffic, and its construction displaced thousands of residents. By the late 2000s, the Sheridan was set with budgetary support from the state to be transformed into a street-level boulevard to alleviate truck traffic, reconnect the community, and open up land for development (prattcenter.net/projects/sustainable-community-development /transforming-sheridan-corridor; Meyer, "Sheridan Expressway").

While MOM pushed for changes that would make residential life in the South Bronx less hazardous, CAAAV organized in the Lower East Side to ensure that city efforts to revitalize the postindustrial waterfront were in the best interests of its community. In 2008, CAAAV and other local community groups such as Good Old Lower East Side along with the progressive Urban Justice Center's Community Development Project formed the Organizing and Uniting Residents Waterfront coalition. That summer, coalition members conducted a survey of eight hundred residents of the Lower East Side and Chinatown about current community concerns and about what residents would like to see included in a newly developed waterfront. During the August 2008 Chinatown Community Struggle event, Chinatown Tenants Union youth members surveyed visitors in addition to presenting their own analyses of housing concerns in Chinatown. Organizing and Uniting Residents Waterfront member groups also hosted three community visioning sessions, during which the member groups offered an overview of the history of the East River waterfront, outlined the proposed development by the city, and conducted small-group conversations among participants. I attended one of these sessions and observed that residents were encouraged to reflect on how they wanted to see the waterfront used as well as what they wanted for their community. Groups were encouraged to pick issues that they were especially interested in and then to build consensus about their priorities. A final town hall meeting drew eighty residents at which they discussed developing a people's plan for the East River waterfront. The plan was to draw on the responses of community members while supplementing their input with financial and business analyses provided by the Pratt Center for Community Development. The main emphasis of the resulting plan was on free and low-cost services, including educational programming for adults and children. It called for the "conversion of Piers 35, 36, and 42 into useable community public space." In the 2010s, much of the plan was enacted as the city developed the area for public use (nycedc.com/project /east-river-waterfront-esplanade). While the area's low-income residents continued to face significant threats from high-end developers, CAAAV and its allies were able to ensure that this public space was one for all the neighborhood's residents rather than just for the wealthy or tourists, as had happened in other areas that were revitalized such as South Street Seaport; they also continued to publicly challenge development plans that would prioritize luxury housing over the needs of existing community members.

CAAAV found itself responding to the immediate needs of the community in the wake of Hurricane Sandy in 2012 and the police shooting of Akai Gurley in 2014. In the first case, Chinatown residents were in desperate need of basic supplies and electricity. The governmental response was lackluster, so CAAAV opened up its Hester Street office to serve people. With almost a thousand volunteers, CAAAV members collected and distributed water, flashlights, batteries, and food (Rivas, "NYC's Chinatown Devastated"). A *Nation* video documented their work, and as executive director Helena Wong observed, there was a striking difference between the help residents were receiving in the area versus the help Wall Street was receiving. She said, "Income and race have a lot to do with the situation that we're in. I went by Wall Street last night and all the lights were on, the buildings were empty, there were christmas lights on the trees and it was absolutely crazy because we had just left here [Chinatown] and it was pitch black" (Rivas, "NYC's Chinatown Devastated"). CAAAV took up queer motherwork praxis to meet the basic needs of a community that was being failed by government supports, engaging with residents where necessary in native Asian languages as well as Spanish (APEN, "Hurricane Sandy"). CAAAV's efforts made it possible for residents to stay in their homes and not be displaced by the disaster.

While Sandy highlighted CAAAV's ability to support the communities of Chinatown and the Lower East Side, its response to the police shooting death of Akai Gurley in a Brooklyn public housing building by Peter Liang, an Asian American police officer, put the organization into direct conflict with members of New York Asian communities (Tracy et al., "NYPD Cop"). CAAAV activists stayed true to their past and continuing participation in anti-police-violence work and cross-racial coalitions in the tradition of activists like Yuri Kochiyama and Grace Lee Boggs. Their queer motherwork commitment to the safety of all communities of color resulted in their being accused of being traitors, as some Chinese community members sought to defend Liang (Yin, "In a Black-and-White"). Such advocates argued that racism was at play in Liang's case because he was found guilty of an offense that few officers had been held accountable for in the past. CAAAV's executive director, Cathy Dang, instead understood the case as a test of their commitment to racial justice: "This is a story and a case that will go down in the history of New York and of race relations in the US. . . . The question is: do we really want to become the oppressor?" (Wong, "'Scapegoated?'"). CAAAV thus stayed firm in its commitment to combatting police brutality, despite the fractious nature of Liang's case.

CAAAV had previously organized many rallies and protests around such killings, including the 1995 shooting death of youth Yong Xin Huang by police in Chinatown, a case that according to journalist Tomio Geron, was "what some consider to be the highest profile case of anti-Asian violence since Vincent Chin" ("New York Story," 1). CAAAV supported his family's and the community's efforts to pressure the district attorney to prosecute Huang's killer (New York Times, "Settlement Reached"). This case, like many others brought by the Brooklyn district attorney, failed to result in even an indictment of the shooters. However, a federal civil suit against New York City resulted in a settlement for his family, suggesting some admission of responsibility for the killing by the city. Along with responding to Chin's, Huang's, and Bell's killings, the group also helped organize the mass protests following other cases when accused police officers were acquitted, such as in that of Amadou Diallo (CAAAV, "Police Brutality"; Lee, "Asian Power").

After Gurley was killed, CAAAV partnered with Asian Americans United (Philadelphia), Chinatown Community for Equitable Development (Los Angeles), the Chinese Progressive Association (San Francisco), and Chinese Progressive Association (Boston) to publicly support Gurley's family (Rankin, "Asian-American Coalition"). While CAAAV was not alone, its stance put it at odds with other New York City Asian groups such as the Chinese Action Network that raised funds for Liang's defense. CAAAV members stood firm against what they identified as a reckless killing of a young Black man in his own public housing building, maintaining their commitment to groups like the Peoples' Justice for Community Control and Police Accountability. As executive director Cathy Dang's public letter noted, "CAAAV, along with the hundreds of thousands of people who have taken the streets, are demanding an overhaul of this system. #BlackLivesMatter and we will not stand for the loss of Black life, dignity, and opportunity at the hands of the state. We hope you will join us to demand justice for Akai Gurley #ThisStopsToday #BlackLivesMatter #ShutIt-Down" (Dang, "CAAAV Statement"). Her words directly situated CAAAV's within the broader Black Lives Matter movement as well as the older anti-police-violence movement that CAAAV had been part of for decades. Moreover, in connecting all forms of state violence that harm the Black community and that CAAAV had sought to address within New York's Asian and broader communities of color, her words convey a queer motherhood perspective.

These series of issues underscore that for groups such as CAAAV and MOM, fighting for low-income New Yorkers' right to safe and affordable housing requires an intersectional approach to both identities and problems. CAAAV and MOM activists sought out coalitions and remained committed to the core values of their groups. Their queer motherwork has allowed New York's low income and residents of color to continue to lay claim to their right to the city despite ongoing economic inequality and the drive to build a New York made up of luxury condos and amenities.

Identity Politics and Intersectionalities in Social Justice Praxis

> Certainly, identity politics has limitations, just as community organizing does ... But these limitations are not secret to activists from these communities, who consistently work to weave together the threads of different constituencies and issues.
>
> SEN, *STIR IT UP*

> People just throw out the phrase "identity politics" as if that is a means of stopping all of the conversation. But you know we have identities and it's okay to embrace those identities and to talk about how our identity shapes us and affects how we move through the world....
> This is our lives that we're talking about, don't be so dismissive of it.
>
> ROXANE GAY, "WRITER ROXANE GAY"

Identity Politics Narratives

Debates about identity politics continue to rage in the contemporary United States, as it is seen as a root cause of social tensions. Invocations of identity politics often fail to differentiate between, say, the Black Lives Matter movement and Iowa U.S. representative Steve King's defense of white supremacy, conflating them as simplistic expressions of identity rather than considering the particularities of how and why identity is being singled out. It is critical to consider how identity connects to lived realities. Black Lives Matters' efforts to address the ongoing disproportionate use of deadly violence by police against Black people is distinct from a right-wing politics that is comfortable with an embrace of "white nationalist, white supremacist, Western civilization" (Gabriel, "Before Trump"). As Rinku Sen points out, activists do not mindlessly deploy these categories, experiences, and histories. My usage of queer motherwork highlights why identity continues to matter for activists seeking to support their community's efforts to secure justice and their future.

117

The dismissal of activists' evocation of an identity-based analysis of social justice issues that Roxane Gay notes is buttressed by a questioning of activists' very ability to think critically. An example of this can be seen in right-wing pundits' attack on the Brown family after the fatal 2014 shooting of Black youth Michael Brown by a white police officer in Ferguson, Missouri. They sought to use the family as a way to disrupt calls for justice by the emerging Black Lives Matter movement. This backlash targeted his parents, who were described as having inferior "intellects, character, and morality" and as "un-thinking puppets serving the interests of 'myriad influence-peddlers'" and "outside agitators" (Itagaki, *Civil Racism*, 221). Similarly, as Parkland, Florida, students gained traction as public figures responding to gun violence, their ability to advocate for themselves came into question. Groups like the National Rifle Association circulated a talking point about youth being manipulated by outside interests. Todd Starnes adopted this same tactic in a Fox News opinion piece: "Honestly, we can't fault the kids. They have been through an unimaginable ordeal, and long before that, their minds were poisoned by liberals who believe there's something wrong with the Second Amendment ("CNN, MSNBC"). The right invoked racist and ageist stereotypes in this cases in an attempt to remove these activists from the public debate about police brutality and gun violence, respectively. In particular, their ability to think critically for themselves was questioned. The very capacity to have, share, and act on one's own knowledge can be undermined through these identity-based smears that simultaneously disavow the need to address identity-based inequities.

These attempts to shut down activists echo the challenges groups like MOM and CAAAV have faced and also highlight the violence that has been part of their histories. Moreover, both the Brown case and the Parkland case demonstrate how questions of power and identity are central to queer motherwork practices. In the first instance, the Brown family's attempts to communicate their pain and point of view were disparaged. Despite the popular rhetoric of family values, their own response to the loss of their child was dismissed, while the defense of aggressive, armed policing was put above the defense of a teenager's life. Nonetheless, a broader movement has taken up the issue of police brutality and refuses to back down. As youth emerge as leaders in both Black Lives Matter and the anti–gun violence movement, they are showing their potential to take part in motherwork themselves.

While attacks against activists by right-wing advocates and media outlets may not come as a surprise, critiques of identity politics have emerged from other corners of the political spectrum as well. For example, political scientist Mark Lilla's 2017 well-publicized *The Once and Future Liberal* criticizes identity politics based on assumptions about a robust "we" that reflects democratic principles versus an insular and destructive "I"-focused identity politics. On this view, it is not a failure of U.S. democracy to include all people in its laws and policies equitably that is most troubling but an unwillingness on the part of activists who organize vis-à-vis identity-based social issues to embrace a mainstream, unmarked claim to citizenship. Lilla concludes his book by returning to "the bubble" rhetoric of university life, an "unreal world" inside campuses that contrasts with the "real world" that exists just outside the university's walls. He claims that 1960s campus radicals were oriented to issues "out there," unlike their contemporary counterparts who are supposedly so "obsessed with their personal identities and campus pseudopolitics that they have much less interest in, less engagement with, and frankly less knowledge of the great *out there*" (139).

However, the same was said of activists in the 1960s at the time, according to sociologist Francesca Polletta: "Scholarly observers were skeptical, sometimes downright dismissive [of college activists]. Student protesters were driven by a 'romantic primitivism' that was irrational, incoherent and susceptible to demagoguery" (*Freedom*, 5–6). By overlooking the debates that surrounded this presumed golden age of activism, Lilla is able to recycle denigrating descriptions of students and to make them seem infantile in comparison to their predecessors.

This fantasy 1960s campus culture ignores fields like ethnic studies and women's studies that came out of this political moment. Such fields ask questions about how issues play both "out there" and on campus. Lilla assumes that prior to the development of these fields, academia provided "a relatively nonpartisan education" (140), an assumption that ignores the explicitly political nature of higher education and its ties to nation building and imperialism, particularly the extent to which higher education was funded and disseminated knowledge to support these efforts. Moreover, there was long overt hostility toward nonmajoritarian faculty and students; women were excluded, there were quotas to limit Jewish enrollment, and there were anti-Communist blacklists. The ivory tower trope also fails to acknowledge the overt influence of the Koch brothers' investments, politicians' efforts to limit academic inquiry, and collaborations with community partners ranging from nonprofits to private industries and governmental agencies. Furthermore, inequity such as the rampant participation of colleges and universities in gentrification and land grabs across the country to the detriment of low-income communities and the explosion of sexual harassment claims by women graduate students and faculty, demonstrate that these institutions are "out there" in the real world and struggle with the same issues that trouble other workplaces.

Lilla connects his concerns about what is occurring in higher education to a broader context by deploying social justice icons. He argues that they would have been failed by "an identity-based education. And it is difficult to imagine them becoming who they became had they been cursed with one. . . . Their education had developed in them a feeling of democratic solidarity" (139). As examples, he invokes Angela Davis, who, he notes, "studied Western philosophy)," along with Elizabeth Cady Stanton and Martin Luther King Jr. (139). Lilla seems to be unaware of or disinterested in what thoughts Davis herself has shared in this current political moment about identity. Her 2016 essay collection *Freedom Is a Constant Struggle* offers a clear sense of her approach. "I find it so interesting," she observes, "that certain moments in the Black freedom struggle can be very easily incorporated into a larger narrative of the struggle for democracy in this country, and then there are others that get completely ignored" (123).

Davis points to the broad agenda of the Black Panther Party's Ten-Point Program that included access to free health care and an end to the incarceration of Black men (122). This history is part of an ongoing movement that is still seeking to create a new world that addresses identity-based injustices. The politics Davis claims, particularly as a scholar whose affiliations include feminist studies, are based in a dynamic understanding of identity. She discusses the perceived tensions between the Black movement and the women's movement, arguing that there is a need "to understand the intersections and interconnections between the two movements. We are still faced with the challenge of understanding the complex ways race, class, gender, sexuality, nation, and ability are intertwined—but also how we move beyond these categories to understand the interrelationships of ideas and processes that seem to be separate and unrelated (4)."

While, in this instance, Davis uses the verb "move" in a manner that could seem like she is suggesting identities must be acknowledged and then set aside, in other places in the collection she suggests ways that identity politics connects with a broad-based social justice movement. Davis claims that there needs to be a transnational "understanding of what feminists often call 'intersectionality.' Not so much intersectionality of identities, but intersectionality of struggles" (144). In this formulation, thinking through identities is not the end goal but instead part of a social praxis through which activists witness and respond to the connections across social justice struggles. Part of this approach necessitates taking identities seriously, as the work of groups like CAAAV and MOM makes clear. Their histories demonstrate at once how different social issues converge and how at times communities and activists can find themselves at cross-purposes due to differences in identities, politics, or analyses.

CAAAV and MOM activists attended events like the 2006 Jews for Racial and Economic Justice's Purim without Papers in support of immigrants' rights as well as participated in the Right to the City alliance and other formal commitments. Their shared vision for a New York that valued their communities brought them together repeatedly, demonstrating that intersectionality in practice is not only about individuals and communities but also about the issues that cross boundaries and feed into each other. Key concerns that are highlighted in *Pushing Back*—housing, domestic work, environmental justice, and police violence—are connected in the lives of community members as well as in the social, political, and economic context that perpetuate injustices. For example, housing issues are tied to decisions about how land is used and maintained, from luxury condos to parks and waste disposal sites, to the policing of communities, and to real wages and low-income workers in fields like domestic work. These issues are long-standing, as neighborhoods in areas like the South Bronx have faced decades of environmental burdens, home demolition for infrastructure projects, and neglect. Racist state violence has been a hallmark of U.S. policing, from the Texas Rangers' lynchings during the turn of the twentieth century to Chicago detective commander Jon Burge's torture squad from the 1970s to 1990s. Domestic workers have been organizing for generations to gain legal rights protections and claim the dignity of their work. The longer histories of these issues have allowed contemporary activists to more fully understand the challenges that their communities face. Importantly, as New York City became increasingly unaffordable and the needs of the affluent were prioritized over poor and low-income residents, activists powerfully contested these inequities. Groups like MOM and CAAAV organized and developed analyses of these social issues, and their embrace of connections reflected the shift in contemporary social justice movement organizing toward a robust use of intersectionality.

It is important to recognize that efforts to build intersectional mobilizations can be challenged by biases and conflicts between communities. The antisemitism within the Women's March leadership serves as an excellent example of such biases and how they can begin to be productively addressed. The Women's March responded to the backlash by bringing on more Jewish leadership, particularly Jewish women of color whose presence had frequently been erased in discussions of race and Judaism in the United States; by so doing, they were able to garner some renewed support from Jewish leftists. Journalist Nylah Burton's coverage for *The Nation* included interviews with organizational leaders and her own reflections as a Black Jewish woman. She described how "it was devastating to watch as an opportunity for real dialogue and exchange, for the hard work of truly intersectional feminism, was sacrificed to the worst impulses of call-out culture" ("Vital"). "Call-out culture" refers to the quick denunciation of people for real or perceived bias, which has been critiqued by activists on the left; instead of finding ways to constructively address such failings and the biases that all people have, call-outers are quick to write off anyone whose politics are not pure. Burton decided to reach out to the women leaders who had been charged with making antisemitic remarks; she didn't know what to expect, but she found that they "readily admitted and apologized for the harm they caused to the Jewish community and to others who felt alienated by their delayed responses to concerns of anti-Semitism" ("Vital") and took the time to get educated more deeply about shared experiences of bigotry across communities.

One high profile leader was Tamika Mallory, a Black woman who had been attacked for engaging with the Nation of Islam's Louis Farrakhan. In a dialogue with Jewish leaders, they conveyed to her that they would not simply reject her, and she observed that "I learned about the duality of being [black and Jewish], dealing with anti-Semitism and anti-black racism at the same time. I learned how to think and speak about [these issues] better and advocate for the people who are affected by this kind of hate" ("Vital"). As a result of coming to recognize that some people live these two experiences daily and that they are shared struggles, Mallory expanded her understanding and made connections that were being ignored in framings of the issue as Black versus Jewish. Another Women's March leader, Linda Sarsour, a Palestinian American leader who has often been attacked, stated that "we unequivocally have rejected the comments made by Minister Farrakhan on LGBTQ communities and on Jewish communities" (Oster, "On Day of Women's March"). Through her precise language, Sarsour reaffirmed the platform of the Women's March and rather than attacking Farrakhan as a figure targeted the language itself that was antagonistic to these communities. As white woman leader Bob Bland observed, "Unity is not uniformity. How else are we going to transform power and learn from each other if we all have the same opinions?" ("Vital"). In this manner, these leaders sought to create room for mistakes, differences, and dialogue that could address these and future conflicts.

While Mark Lilla reads identity-based activism as disruptive of democracy, I argue that the Womens' March drama alongside the work of groups like MOM and CAAAV demonstrates that true democratic practice requires naming, honesty, and generative conflict as well as solidarity work. Angela Davis and others suggest that the work of digging into how oppression functions vis-à-vis identity is necessary to pursuing justice as a democratic practice. As ethics scholar Antonia Darder puts it, we must have "a clear recognition that cultural and linguistic differences are absolutely vital and necessary to the perpetuation of human life, just as moments of political dissent are essential to the continuing evolution of our democratic existence" (quoted in Jobin-Leeds and AgitArte, *When We Fight We Win*, 166). Rather than asking, as some do, that activists homogenize their identities and, by extension, their political perspectives, scholar-activists like Davis and Darder recognize that it is through knowing oneself and finding connections across and within differences that social justice movements are able to flourish today.

ACKNOWLEDGMENTS

Thank you to all of the activists that have been and are part of MOM and CAAAV, and their ally groups. Your knowledge, generosity, passion, and kindness have made it possible for me to pursue this project. Thank you especially to Nova Strachan, Wanda Salaman, Sung E. Bai, Helena Wong, Carolyn De Leon, Maria Rivera, Chhaya Choum, Esther Wong, Carmen Silva, Wilfredo Febre, Thoul Tong, Taleigh Smith, Thomas Assefa, Mark Swier, Revital Aranbaev, Catrina Davis, Cerita Parker, Laurel Turbin, Shaun Lin, Lydia Velez, Cathy Dang, Nita Asuncion, Inday Baldivia, Star Dungo, Josie Rumna, and Nancy Ventic. I have had many invaluable conversations with all of you. I found that so many CAAAV and MOM activists were not only willing to share their knowledge and experiences with me but also engage and support me in ways that I could not have anticipated. For all I have learned and for allowing me to be part of your worlds, thank you. I hope that this book adequately shares some of what I have learned from you and your many accomplishments.

My path into higher education has been deeply rewarding and challenging. Thank you to the many mentors I have been fortunate to find along the way. I am grateful to John D'Emilio, Jennie Brier, and Lynette Jackson for patiently working with me as an undergraduate and continuing to support me as I develop as a scholar. Thank you also to Elena Gutiérrez, Sandra Bartky, Jamie Hovey, Jennifer Langdon, and Gayatri Reddy. You all enabled me to pursue an undergraduate education at University of Illinois–Chicago that changed my life for the better, intellectually and personally. I learned much about our world and benefited from your dynamic pedagogy. I appreciate the deep commitment to teaching alongside research and activism that you all demonstrated and that drew me into the field of gender and women's studies.

At Rutgers, I benefited from excellent faculty. Nancy Hewitt has been a generous teacher and mentor, showing a deep capacity for intellectual rigor alongside kindness and humor. Barbara Balliet was an endless support and mentor in all elements of university life. Judy Gerson's engagement with me throughout my studies empowered me to fully step into the role of researcher. Robyn Rodriguez was generous in sharing her knowledge and encouragement for my project. The broader faculty in Women's and Gender Studies provided me with a training that I am grateful for every day I step into the classroom or pick up a piece of scholarship. My thanks to these faculty members as well as Carlos Decena, Arlene Stein, Charlotte Bunch, Ana Yolanda Ramos-Zayas, Jasbir Puar, Louisa Schein, Harriet Davidson, Leslie McCall, and Elizabeth

Grosz. Other members of the Rutgers community also served as great mentors and colleagues including Beth Hutchison, Mary Hawkesworth, Temma Kaplan, Cheryl Clarke, Anna Sampaio, Yana Rodgers, Ethel Brooks, Nikol Alexander-Floyd, Lisa Hetfield, Mary Trigg, Sasha Taner, Gail Reilly, Jewel Daney, Ria Das Gupta, Nathalie Margie, Mary Jane Real, Desiree Ficula, Margot Baruch, and Marlene Importico. Thank you to Joanne Givand and Suzy Kiefer for providing so much personal support as well as administrative skill throughout my studies. Kayo Denda has been an amazing librarian and colleague, patiently teaching me new skills and sharing resources while always conveying an enthusiasm for research and teaching.

Thank you to the students I have taught at Rutgers University and Connecticut College. Your questions and ideas have helped me think differently about my research, pushing me to challenge assumptions and make new connections. Thank you particularly to the students who have worked with me on this project: Joey Mercado, Samantha Pevear, Flor Campos, Ally Ang, Kali Guise, Deven Stahl, Hanako Brais, and Kori Rimany. You all have helped move the work itself along as well as remind me of how amazing it is that I have this opportunity.

I am thankful for many classmates, neighbors, and activists who became mentors, colleagues, and friends during my time at University of Illinois–Chicago and Rutgers. Thank you particularly to Carl T. Wilson, Kandy Christensen, Stephanie Gentry-Fernandez, Araceli Martinez, Tania Unzueta, Elsa Mitsoglou, Ana Turck, Rachael Dietkus, Anna Batcke, Nancy Hernandez, Jorge Valdivia, Ivan Torrijos, Edgar Rivera Colón and the entire Rivera Colón family, Anahi Russo, Danielle Phillips, Agatha Beins, Elaine Zundl, Mariana Cruz, Chelsea Booth, Debarati Sen, Eunsung Lee, Kelly Coogan, Andy Mazzaschi, Kathleen Powers, Gwen Kash, Rebecca Coleman, Namita Chad, Doña Maria Baez, and Wilfredo Ortiz.

I have had the good fortune of finding a home at Connecticut College. R. Danielle Egan has provided inspiration and support for taking productive risks with my research and teaching. Lisa Wilson, MaryAnne Borrelli, Joan Chrisler, and Denise Pelletier have gone above and beyond in taking the time to mentor me since my arrival. Andrea Wollensak has been a fantastic collaborator on campus, and I am also deeply indebted to her for the work she has done with me for this book in using her design expertise to develop a dynamic map and figures. Denis Ferhatovic has always brought curiosity and joy to our interactions. Joyce Bennett has modeled professionalism and a passion for our work as faculty. I am thankful to have so many colleagues and friends who have provided me with support and encouragement, including my kind former neighbors, Ginger, Robert, and George, as well as Celestino Sajvin, Chelsea Fennell, Suzuko Knott, Nina Martin, Rosemarie Roberts, Rose Oliveira, Becky Parmer, Kim Sanchez, Greg Post, Pat Lynch, Erin Doheny, Kathy Parker, Barb

Nagy, Sarah Hunt, Vicki Carter, Denisse Olivo, Audrey Zakriski, Rebecca Mc-Cue, Angela Barney, Rachel Spicer, Deb Eastman, Simon Feldman, Erin Duran, Ginny Anderson, Steve Luber, Sabrina Notarfrancisco, Mónika López Anuarbe, Maria Cruz-Saco, Julie Rivkin, Ana Campos Manzo, Leo Garafolo, Ron Flores, Michelle Dunlap, Tricia Dallas, Noel Garrett, Jessica McCullough, Lyndsay Bratton, Candace Howes, Mab Segrest, Shubhra Sharma, and Jenny Bonnano. Thank you also to Dana Wright, Emma Sterrett-Hong, Maria Hantzopoulos, and Lionel Howard for all of your encouraging feedback on my work. Ashley Hanson and Andrew Lopez have contributed much to my research for this project and others; you are both exemplary librarians and colleagues. Thank you all very much.

Thank you to Sara Schley for getting me back on track with this book, I appreciate your straightforward, entertaining, and kind approach to mentoring. Thank you to the Connecticut College Dean of Faculty for supporting my participation in the National Center for Faculty Development and Diversity Faculty Success Program. It has allowed me to better manage challenges and continue moving forward in my work. Thank you to Annelise Orleck, Tamar Carroll, and Eileen Boris for your generous mentoring on this project and others.

Thank you to Renee Romano and Claire Potter for seeing the potential of this project. Renee provided impactful feedback as I reworked the initial material for the book. Lynn Itagaki has taken up working with me with a generous spirit. Her expertise and incisive questions have drawn out the core ideas of this book much further than I could have hoped. Mick Gusinde-Duffy has been a stalwart supporter of my project throughout the process. My thanks to Mick and his team, particularly Bethany Snead and Kaelin Broaddus, for your generous and kind work with me.

Thank you to Sarah Grey for working with me on the early versions of this book. Your input helped me think differently about its content and clarify my ideas. Summar West has thoughtfully provided editorial feedback that further elucidates my thoughts and focuses my words throughout the book. I greatly appreciate MJ Devaney's deep and careful work with my manuscript. My gratitude to Samantha Marble for permission to reproduce her powerful image of Lisa Ramirez for *Exit Cuckoo*.

I am thankful for the support I received throughout this project's life from my dissertation research to this book's publication. At Rutgers University, I benefited from support through the Department of Women's and Gender Studies, the Graduate School, the Institute for Research on Women, the Rutgers Center for Historical Analysis, and the Institute for Women's Leadership. At Connecticut College, funding from the Dean of Faculty's Office, the Research Matters Fund, the R. F. Johnson Faculty Development Fund, the Judith Tindal Opartny '72 Junior Faculty Fellows Fund, and the Center for the Comparative Study of Race and Ethnicity grant have all contributed to this book.

My family has provided critical support throughout my education and career. I greatly appreciate their belief in my research as well as in my ability to pursue this path. Pamela and George Rotramel have been parents who have demonstrated a deep love for me and appreciation for my interests. Alizah Rotramel has always encouraged me through the ups and downs of this life. Thank you also to Bryan Chang, Wei Shih, and our newest family member, Rivka Chang, for their love and support. I am grateful too that my family has expanded to include the Rodriguez-Beltran-Perez-Solivan clan. I appreciate the interest that you all have shown in my work and your patient encouragement as I move along. Thank you for welcoming me with such loving and joyous spirit. Also, a special shout out to furry friends past and present—Bruce, Max, Precious, Stu, Pablo (the reptilian exception), Ben and Jerry, Ellie, Tippi, Jordan, Mozilla, and more have all been such fun. Finally, thank you to my love, Dianna Rodriguez. It is an honor to be your partner and to share this journey with you. I value deeply your care, wisdom, generosity, commitment, curiosity, ethics, and humor. Thank you for all of your patience, openness, support, and love.

Organizations and Their Activities

MOTHERS ON THE MOVE/MADRES EN MOVIMIENTO (MOM)

Environmental Justice campaign
Tenants Rallying in Unity to Maintain Public Housing
Youth on the Move

CAAAV: ORGANIZING ASIAN COMMUNITIES (FORMERLY THE COMMITTEE AGAINST ANTI-ASIAN VIOLENCE)

Asian Youth in Action
Chinatown Justice Project
Chinatown Tenants Union
Lease Drivers' Coalition
Southeast Asian Organizing Collective-Youth Leadership Project
Women Workers Project

ALLIED ORGANIZATIONS

ACT UP
Asian Americans United (Philadelphia)
Chinatown Community for Equitable Development (Los Angeles)
Chinese Progressive Association (Boston)
Chinese Progressive Association (San Francisco)
Audre Lorde Project (ALP)
Bronx Youth Community Organization (BYCO)
Crotona Community Coalition
Domestic Workers United (DWU)
Fabulous Independent Educated Radicals for Community Empowerment (FIERCE)
Families United for Racial and Economic Equality (FUREE)
Foundry Theatre
Gay Men of African Descent
Jews for Racial and Economic Justice (JFREJ)
Las Buenas Amigas
Latino Gay Men of New York
Natural Resources Defense Council
Nodutdol for Korean Community Development
Northwest Bronx Community and Clergy Coalition (NWBCCC)
NYC Alliance to Preserve Public Housing
Organization for Asian Women
Peoples' Justice for Community Control and Police Accountability

Queer Nation
Right to the City Alliance
Salsa Soul Sisters
Service Employees International Union
South Asian Lesbians and Gay Men (SALGA)
Sustainable South Bronx (SSBX)
Sylvia Rivera Law Project (SRLP)
Working Theater

BIBLIOGRAPHY

Acosta, Jose. "Aquí no hay quien respire." *El Diario/La Prensa*, March 26, 2008, 4.

ATSDR [Agency for Toxic Substances and Disease Registry]. ATSDR *Case Studies in Environmental Triggers of Asthm*a. Washington, DC: U.S. Department of Health and Human Services, 2014. atsdr.cdc.gov/csem/asthma/docs/asthma.pdf.

Aguilar-San Juan, Karin, ed. *The State of Asian America: Activism and Resistance in the 1990s*. Boston: South End Press, 1994.

Ahmed, Insanul. "Hunts Point Residents Join Housing March." *Hunts Point Express* (NY), May 25, 2007. brie.hunter.cuny.edu/hpe/2007/05/25/hunts-point-residents-join -housing-march.

Akchurin, Maria, and Cheol-Sung Lee. "Pathways to Empowerment: Repertoires of Women's Activism and Gender Earnings Equality." *American Sociological Review* 78, no. 4 (2013): 679–701.

Alexander, Michelle. *The New Jim Crow: Mass Incarceration in the Age of Colorblindness*. New York: New Press, 2010.

Alexander, Priscilla. Letter to the Editor. *New York Times*, July 18, 1994. nytimes.com /1994/07/18/opinion/l-women-in-prison-don-t-get-equal-treatment-crackdown -to-backfire-700703.html.

Alexander-Floyd, Nikol G. "Disappearing Acts: Reclaiming Intersectionality in the Social Sciences in a Post-Black Feminist Era." *Feminist Formations* 24, no. 1 (2012): 1–25.

Allison, Dorothy. "A Question of Class." In *Skin: Talking about Sex, Class and Literature*, 13–36. Ann Arbor, MI: Firebrand Books, 1994.

Anderson, Benedict. *Imagined Communities*. New York: Verso, 2006.

Antrobus, Peggy. *The Global Women's Movement: Origins, Issues and Strategies for the New Century*. London: Zed Books, 2004.

———. "Transformational Leadership: Advancing the Agenda for Gender Justice." *Gender and Development* 8, no. 3 (November 2000): 50–56.

Anzaldúa, Gloria. "Del Otro Lado." In *Compañeras: Latina Lesbians*, edited by Juanita Ramos, 2–3. New York: Latina Lesbian History Project, 1994.

Asian American Federation. "New 2010 Census Data Show Increasing Diversity in New York City's Asian Community." Press Release, July 14, 2011. aafederation.org /press/pressrelease.asp?prid=126&y=2011.

APEN [Asian Pacific Environmental Network]. "CAAAV's Hurricane Sandy Relief." *Asian Pacific Environmental Network Blog*, December 5, 2012. apen4ej.org/caaavs -hurricane-sandy-relief.

Assefa, Thomas. "Noxious Sludge Stench in New York City." *Sludge News*. September 8, 2008. sludgenews.org/action/story.aspx?id=62.

Bald, Vivek. *Bengali Harlem and the Lost Histories of South Asian America*. Cambridge, MA: Harvard University Press, 2013.

Barbarino, Al. "Chinatown Residents Protest against Landlords, Complaining of Bad Conditions, Harassment," *Daily News* (NY), May 9, 2011. nydailynews.com /new-york/chinatown-residents-protest-landlords-complaining-bad-conditions -harassment-article-1.143417.

Barr, Alistair. "SoHo, New York: Mixed Use, Density and the Power of the Myth." Barr Gazetas Architects London, 2007. sohomemory.org/sites/default/files /documents/2018_03_12_documents_informational_SoHo_New_York_Paper _alastair_barr_nd.pdf.

Bauman, Zygmunt. *Wasted Lives: Modernity and its Outcasts*. Malden, MA: Polity Press, 2004.

Beekman, Daniel. "The Changing Chinatowns: Move over Manhattan, Sunset Park Now Home to Most Chinese in NYC," *Daily News* (NY), August 5, 2011. nydailynews.com /changing-chinatowns-move-manhattan-sunset-park-home-chinese-nyc-article -1.948028.

Bobadilla, Suzanna. "The Feministing Five: ManSee Kong." *Feministing*, May 24, 2014. feministing.com/2014/05/24/the-feministing-five-mansee-kong.

Boris, Eileen, and Premilla Nadasen. "Domestic Workers Organize!" *Working USA: The Journal of Labor and Society* 11, no. 4 (D2008): 413–37.

Boris, Eileen, and Rhacel Salazar Parreñas. *Intimate Labors: Cultures, Technologies, and the Politics of Care*. Stanford, CA: Stanford University Press, 2010.

Brash, Julian. *Bloomberg's New York: Class and Governance in the Luxury City*. Athens: University of Georgia Press, 2011.

Brecher, Charles, and Raymond D. Horton with Robert A. Cropf and Dean Michael Mead. *Power Failure: New York City Politics and Policy since 1960*. New York: Oxford University Press, 1993.

Briggs, Laura. *Reproducing Empire: Race, Sex, Science, and U.S. Imperialism in Puerto Rico*. Berkeley: University of California Press, 2002.

Brown, Elsa Barkley. "'What Has Happened Here': The Politics of Difference in Women's History and Feminist Politics." *Feminist Studies* 18, no. 2 (1992): 295–312.

Brown, Wendy. "Wounded Attachments." *Political Theory* 21, no. 3 (1993): 390–410.

Brownstoner. "Closing Bell: Tenants File Lawsuit Against NYCHA." Brownstoner, March 1, 2012. brownstoner.com/blog/2012/03/closing-bell-tenants-call-out -nycha.

Brunkhorst, Hauke. "Global Society as the Crisis in Democracy." In *The Transformation of Modernity: Aspects of the Past, Present, and Future of an Era*, edited By Mikael Carleheden and Michael Hviid Jacobsen, 225–40. Burlington, VT: Ashgate, 2001.

Burton, Nylah. "A Vital, Vulnerable Conversation With the Leaders of the Women's March." *Nation*. January 18, 2019. thenation.com/article/womens-march-mallory -sarsour-bland-perez.

Calmes, Maggie. "Wary of Gentrification, East Harlem Braces for Rapid Change." *Gotham Gazette* (NY), April 1, 2016. gothamgazette.com/city/6253-wary-of -gentrification-east-harlem-braces-for-rapid-change.

Cannato, Vincent J. *The Ungovernable City: John Lindsay and His Struggle to Save New York*. New York: Basic Books, 2001.

Cantarow, Ellen, with Susan O'Malley and Sharon Hartman Strom. 1980. *Moving the Mountain: Women Working for Social Change*. New York: Feminist Press at the City University of New York.

Carroll, Tamar W. *Mobilizing New York: AIDS, Antipoverty, and Feminist Activism*. Chapel Hill: University of North Carolina Press, 2015.

Casimir, Leslie, and Paul H. B. Shin. "Group Urges Domestics' Bill of Rights," *Daily News* (NY), December 19, 2004.

CBS New York. "Bronx Public Housing Residents Complain Of Rat Infestation." CBS News New York. CBS Broadcasting, Inc., August 16, 2012. newyork.cbslocal .com/2012/08/16/bronx-public-housing-residents-complain-of-rat-infestation.

Center for Constitutional Rights. "Floyd, et al. v. City of New York, et al." ccrjustice .org/floyd.

CDC [Centers for Disease Control and Prevention]. "CDC Health Disparities and Inequalities Report—United States, 2013." *Morbidity and Mortality Weekly Report* 62, no. 3 (2013): 1–186.

Chan, June, Tsuh Yang Chen, Milyoung Cho, and James Jaewhan Lee. "The Pain of *Miss Saigon.*" *OutWeek*, March 13, 1991, 5.

Chen, Michelle. "Democracy Begins at Home: Public Housing Tenants Without a Voice." *ColorLines*, January 23, 2010, colorlines.com/archives/2010/01/democracy _in_public_housing.html.

Cohen, Cathy J. "Punks, Bulldaggers, and Welfare Queens." *GLQ* 3, no. 4 (1997): 437–465
———. "What Is This Movement Doing to My Politics?" *Social Text* 61 (1999): 111–18.

Cohen-Cruz, Jan. *Remapping Performance: Common Ground, Uncommon Partners*. New York: Palgrave Macmillan, 2015.

Colleran, Jeanne, and Jenny S. Spencer. Introduction. In *Staging Resistance: Essays on Political Theater*, edited by Jeanne Colleran and Jenny S. Spencer, 1–12. Ann Arbor: University of Michigan Press, 1998.

Collins, Patricia Hill. *Black Feminist Thought: Knowledge, Consciousness, and the Politics of Empowerment*. New York: Routledge, 1990.
———. "Shifting the Center: Race, Class, and Feminist Theorizing about Motherhood." In *Mothering: Ideology, Experience and Agency*, edited by Evelyn Nakano Glenn, Grace Chang, and Linda Forcey, 45–65. New York: Routledge, 1994.

Collins, Patricia Hill, and Sirma Bilge. *Intersectionality*. Malden, MA: Polity Press, 2016.

Columbia Center for Children's Environmental Health. "Healthy Home Healthy Child: Air Pollution in Your Neighborhood—What's Being Done To Improve It." Mailman School of Public Health, Spring 2005. ccceh.hs.columbia.edu/pdf-newsletter /HHHCspring05eng.pdf.

Combahee River Collective. "The Combahee River Collective Statement." In *How We Get Free: Black Feminism and the Combahee River Collective*, edited by Keeanga -Yamahtta Taylor, 15–27. Chicago: Haymarket Books, 2017.

CAAAV [Committee Against Anti-Asian Violence]. "Asian Man Murdered; Vincent Chin Revisited," CAAAV *Voice*, 1, no. 3 (1989): 2.
———. "CAAAV Expansion—Preparing for the Challenges to Come." CAAAV *Voice* 2, no. 2 (1991): 1, 3.

———. "CAAAV Launches Women Workers Project." CAAAV *Voice* 8, no. 2 (1996): 1, 9.

———. "Police Brutality in the New Chinatown." In *Zero Tolerance: Quality of Life and the New Police Brutality in New York City*, edited by Andrea McArdle and Tanya Erzen, 221–41. New York: New York University Press, 2001.

———. "Right to the City." CAAAV *Voice* 15, no. 2 (Fall 2007): 8–9.

———. "Testimony by Committee Against Anti-Asian Violence, New York." In *Hearing before the Subcommittee on Crime and Criminal Justice, Committee on the Judiciary, House of Representatives, May 11, 1992, 102nd Cong., sess. 2*, 174–84. Washington DC: U.S. Government Printing Office, 1992.

CAAAV [Committee against Anti-Asian Violence] and Urban Justice Center. *Converting Chinatown: A Snapshot of a Neighborhood Becoming Unaffordable and Unlivable*. New York: CAAAV and Urban Justice Center, 2008.

CAAAV [Committee against Anti-Asian Violence], FIERCE [Fabulous Independent Educated Radicals for Community Empowerment], FUREE [Families United for Racial and Economic Equality], and Urban Justice Center. *New York City Anti-Gentrification Network: Summation of Convenings*. New York: CAAAV, FIERCE, FUREE, and Urban Justice Center, 2007. cdp.urbanjustice.org/sites/default/files/NYC_anti_gentrification.pdf.

Constable, Nicole. *Maid to Order in Hong Kong: Stories of Filipina Worker*. Ithaca, NY: Cornell University Press, 1997.

Cook, Nancy. "If the Factory Smells, Is it Environmentally Offensive?" *Z Magazine*, September 2004. zcomm.org/zmagazine/if-the-factory-smells-is-it-environmentally-offensive-by-nancy-cook.

Corey, Matthew. "Despite Popularity, City Speed Humps on Hold." *Norwood News* 11, no. 25 (1999). www.bronxmall.com/norwoodnews/past/123198/news/page3.html.

Crean, Melanie. "Malleable Environments and the Pursuit of Spatial Justice in the Bronx." *Leonardo* 47, no. 4 (2014): 337–43.

Crenshaw, Kimberlé. "Demarginalizing the Intersection of Race and Sex: A Black Feminist Critique of Antidiscrimination Doctrine, Feminist Theory and Antiracist Politics." *University of Chicago Legal Forum* 140 (1989): 139–67.

Culvert Chronicles. "NYC Alliance Rallies to 'Save New York City! Save Public Housing!'" *Culvert Chronicles* (NY), July 1–7, 2010, 18.

Dang, Cathy. "CAAAV Statement to Asian and Asian American Communities on the Murder of Akai Gurley by NYPD Officer Peter Liang." Peoples' Justice for Community Control and Police Accountability, February 13, 2015. peoplesjustice.org/releases/caaav-statement-asian-and-asian-american-communities-murder-akai-gurley-nypd-officer-peter.

Das Gupta, Monisha. *Unruly Immigrants: Rights, Activism, and Transnational South Asian Politics in the United States*. Durham, NC: Duke University Press, 2006.

David, Greg. *Modern New York: The Life and Economics of a City*. New York: Palgrave Macmillan, 2012.

Davis, Angela Y. *Freedom is a Constant Struggle: Ferguson, Palestine, and the Foundations of a Movement*. Chicago: Haymarket Books, 2016.

———. *The Meaning of Freedom, And Other Difficult Dialogues*. San Francisco: City Lights Open Media, 2012.

Dean, Gwendolyn Alden. "Asian Lesbians and Gays Protest Lambda Fund-Raiser." In *Great Events from History: Gay, Lesbian, Bisexual, and Transgender Events, 1848–2006*, edited by Lillian Faderman, 542–45. Hackensack, NJ: Salem Press, 2007.

Deo, Meera E., Jenny J. Lee, Christina B. Chin, Noriko Milman, and Nancy Wang Yuen. "Missing in Action: 'Framing' Race on Prime-Time Television." *Social Justice* 35, no. 2 (2008): 145–62.

DiNapoli, Thomas. *Housing Affordability in New York State*. New York State Office of the State Comptroller, March 2014. osc.state.ny.us/reports/housing/affordable _housing_ny_2014.pdf.

DiNapoli, Thomas, and Kenneth B. Bleiwas. *The Role of Immigrants in the New York City Economy*. New York: New York State Office of the State Comptroller, 2010. osc.state .ny.us/osdc/rpt17–2010.pdfhttps://www.osc.state.ny.us/osdc/rpt17–2010.pdf.

Domestic Workers United. "*Exit Cuckoo*—November 22nd—DWU Fundraiser." DWU Blog, October 22, 2008, http://domesticworkersunited.blogspot.com/2008/10/exit -cuckoo-november-22nd-dwu.html.

Domestic Workers United and DataCenter. *Home Is Where the Work Is: Inside New York's Domestic Work Industry*. Bronx, NY: DataCenter, 2006, datacenter.org /reports/homeiswheretheworkis.pdf.

Domestic Workers United and National Employment Law Project. *Rights Begin at Home: Protecting Yourself as a Domestic Worker*. New York: Domestic Workers United and National Employment Law Project, 2010. nelp.org/wp-content /uploads/2015/03/RightsBeginatHome.pdf.

Douglass, Frederick. "West Indian Emancipation." In *Frederick Douglass: Selected Speeches and Writings*, edited by Philip S. Foner, 358–68. Chicago: Lawrence Hill, 1999.

Dowell, LeiLani. "First Trans Day of Action draws 1,000." Mundo Obrero Workers Word, June 29, 2005. workers.org/2005/us/trans-day-0707.

Dwoskin, Elizabeth. "When Hipsters Move in on Chinese: It's Ugly." *Village Voice*, April 20, 2010. villagevoice.com/2010/04/20/when-hipsters-move-in-on-chinese -its-ugly.

Dzidzienyo, Anani, and Suzanne Oboler, eds. *Neither Enemies nor Friends*. New York: Palgrave Macmillan: 2005.

Egbert, Bill. "Hunts Point Activist Group Raises Stink over Fertilizer Plant." *Daily News* (NY), April 14, 2008. www.nydailynews.com/new-york/bronx/hunts-point -activist-group-raises-stink-fertilizer-plant-article-1.281266.

———. "Protest Victory as State Orders Bronx Fertilizer Firm to Cut Stink," *Daily News* (NY), October 9, 2008. nydailynews.com/new-york/bronx/protest-victory-state -orders-bronx-fertilizer-firm-cut-stink-article-1.301645.

Eide, Stephen. *Poverty and Progress in New York: Conditions in New York City's Poorest Neighborhoods. Civic Report* 88. New York: Center for State and Local Leadership at the Manhattan Institute, 2014. www.manhattan-institute.org/sites/default/files /cr_88.pdf.

Ely, Robin J., Herminia Ibarra, and Deborah Kolb. "Taking Gender Into Account: Theory and Design for Women's Leadership Development Programs." *Academy of Management Learning & Education* 10, no. 3 (2011): 474–93.

Enck-Wanzer, Darrel, ed. *The Young Lords: A Reader*. New York: New York University Press, 2010.

Eng, David L., and Alice Y. Hom. Introduction to *Q & A: Queer in Asian America*. Philadelphia: Temple University Press, 1998.

Feldman, Roberta M., and Susan Stall. *The Dignity of Resistance: Women Residents' Activism in Chicago Public Housing*. New York: Cambridge University Press, 2004.

Ferguson, Roderick A. *Aberrations In Black: Toward A Queer Of Color Critique*. Minneapolis: University of Minnesota Press, 2004.

Fernandes, Leela. "The Politics of Forgetting: Class Politics, State Power and the Restructuring of Urban Space in India." *Urban Studies* 41, no. 12 (2004): 2415–30.

Fessler, Pam. "After Katrina, New Orleans' Public Housing Is a Mix of Pastel and Promises." *NPR*, August 17, 2015. npr.org/2015/08/17/431267040/after-katrina-new -orleans-public-housing-is-a-mix-of-pastel-and-promises.

Findlay, Eileen J. "Slipping and Sliding: The Many Meanings of Race in Life Histories of New York Puerto Rican Return Migrants in San Juan." *Centro Journal* 24, no. 1 (2012): 20–43.

Finger, Davida. "Public Housing in New Orleans Post Katrina: The Struggle for Housing as a Human Right." *Review of Black Political Economy* 38, (2011): 327–37.

Flood, Joe. "Why the Bronx Burned." *New York Post*, May 16, 2010. nypost.com/2010 /05/16/why-the-bronx-burned.

Forero, Juan. "No Longer A War Zone, Hunts Point Gains Status; New Services Arrive as City Improvements Lift Bronx Community." *New York Times*, August 23, 2000. nytimes.com/2000/08/23/nyregion/no-longer-war-zone-hunts-point-gains-status -new-services-arrive-city.html.

Fox News. "Watters' World: Chinatown Edition," October 3, 2016. video.foxnews.com /v/5154040766001.

Freeman, Jo. "The Tyranny of Structurelessness." *WSQ: Women's Studies Quarterly* 41, no. 3 (2013): 231–46.

Fuchs, Chris. "Decades after a Cop Shot Her Brother, Qinglan Huang Speaks Up for Akai Gurley." *NBC News*, April 11, 2016. nbcnews.com/news/asian-america/two -decades-after-cop-shot-her-brother-qing-lan-huang-n554146.

———. "Former NYPD Cop Peter Liang's Guilty Verdict Leaves a Community Divided." *NBC News*, February 13, 2016. nbcnews.com/news/asian-america /former-nypd-cop-peter-liang-s-guilty-verdict-leaves-community-n518056.

Fujino, Diane C. "Who Studies the Asian American Movement?: A Historiographical Analysis." *Journal of Asian American Studies* 11, no. 2 (June 2008): 127–69.

Furman Center for Real Estate and Urban Policy. *State of New York City's Housing and Neighborhoods 2008*. New York: New York University, 2008. furmancenter.org /files/sotc/State_of_the_City_2008.pdf.

Gabriel, Trip. "Before Trump, Steve King Set the Agenda for the Wall and Anti-Immigrant Politics." *New York Times*, January 10, 2019. nytimes.com/2019/01/10/us /politics/steve-king-trump-immigration-wall.html.

Gallagher, Julie A. *Black Women and Politics in New York City*. Urbana: University of Illinois Press, 2012.

Gates, Anita. "Surviving the Mother-Nanny Divide." *New York Times*, April 23, 2009. nytimes.com/2009/04/24/theater/reviews/24exit.html.

Gay, Roxane. "Writer Roxane Gay on Speaking Up, Female Friendship and 'Difficult Women.'" KQED, February 22, 2017. kqed.org/forum/2010101858836/writer-roxane -gay-on-speaking-up-female-friendship-and-difficult-women.

Geron, Tomio. "New York Story: Asian-Asian Violence Wants New Investigation into the Killing of Yong Xin Huang; Shades of Vincent Chin," *AsianWeek* 17, no. 8 (1995).

Giddings, Paula J. *Ida: A Sword among Lions: Ida B. Wells and the Campaign Against Lynching*. New York: Amistad/HarperCollins Publishers, 2008.

Glaeser, Edward L. "Urban Colossus: Why Is New York America's Largest City?" *Economic Policy Review* 11, no. 2 (2005): 7–24.

Glazer, Nathan. "The South-Bronx Story: An Extreme Case of Neighborhood Decline." *Policy Studies Journal* 16, no. 2 (1987): 269–76.

Gold, Roberta. "'I Had Not Seen Women like That Before:' Intergenerational Feminism in New York City's Tenant Movement." *Feminist Studies* 35, no. 2 (2009): 387–415.

———. *When Tenants Claimed the City: The Struggle for Citizenship in New York Housing*. Urbana: University of Illinois Press, 2014.

Gonen, Yoav. "NYC Rents Skyrocket as Incomes Lag." *New York Post*, April 23, 2014. nypost.com/2014/04/23/rising-rents-in-nyc-top-those-in-the-rest-of-the-nation -while-incomes-fail-to-keep-up.

Gonzalez, Evelyn Diaz. *The Bronx*. New York: Columbia University Press, 2004.

Goodman, J. David. "De Blasio Expands Affordable Housing, but Results Aren't Always Visible." *New York Times*, October 5, 2017. nytimes.com/2017/10/05/nyregion /de-blasio-affordable-housing-new-york-city.html?_r=0.

Goodstein, Steven. "Piano District Name Stems Back to Neighborhood's Roots." *Bronx Times*, January 24, 2016. www.bxtimes.com/stories/2016/4/04-pianodistrict-2016 -01-22-bx.html.

Green, Rodney D., Marie Kouassi, and Belinda Mambo. "Housing, Race, and Recovery from Hurricane Katrina." *Review of Black Political Economy* 40, no. 1 (2013): 145–63.

Grieve, Ev. "The *Times* Discovers Chinatown." Ev Grieve Blog, September 18, 2008. evgrieve.com/2008/09/times-discovers-chinatown.html.

Grossman, Jill. "Banana Kelly Gets a New Bunch." *City Limits*, November 11, 2002. www .citylimits.org/news/articles/873/banana-kelly-gets-a-new-bunch.

Guglielmo, Jennifer. *Living the Revolution: Italian Women's Resistance and Radicalism in New York City, 1880–1945*. Chapel Hill: University of North Carolina Press, 2010.

Guillermo, Emil. "Vincent Chin? Remembering Ronald Ebens—The Guy Who Got away with Murder." Asian American Legal Defense and Education Fund, June 13, 2011. aaldef.org/blog/vincent-chin-remembering-ronald-ebens-the-guy-who-got -away-with-murder.html.

Haedicke, Susan C., and Tobin Nellhaus. introduction to *Performing Democracy: International Perspectives on Urban Community-Based Performance*, edited by Susan C. Haedicke and Tobin Nellhaus, 1–24. Ann Arbor: University of Michigan Press, 2001.

Hall, Stuart, ed. *Cultural Representations and Signifying Practices*. London: Open
    University Press, 1997.
Haraway, Donna. "Situated Knowledges: The Science Question in Feminism and the
    Privilege of Partial Perspective." *Feminist Studies* 14, no. 3 (1988): 575–99.
Harvey, David. "The Right to the City." *New Left Review* 53 (): 23–40.
Hawkesworth, Mary. "Global Containment: The Production of Feminist Invisibility and
    the Vanishing Horizon of Justice." In *Rethinking Globalism*, edited by Manfred B.
    Steger, 51–65. Lanham, MD: Rowman and Littlefield, 2004.
Hewitt, Nancy A. Introduction to *No Permanent Waves: Recasting Histories of U.S.
    Feminism*, edited By Nancy A. Hewitt, 1–13. Piscataway, NJ: Rutgers University Press,
    2010.
———. *Southern Discomfort: Women's Activism in Tampa, Florida, 1880s-1920s*. Urbana:
    University of Illinois Press, 2001.
Hicks, Jonathan P. "Budget Battleground: Funds for the Young." *New York Times*, May 30,
    1994. nytimes.com/1994/05/30/nyregion/budget-battleground-funds-for-the
    -young.
———. "Giuliani Broadens Crackdown To Banish All Illegal Vendors." *New York Times*,
    May 9, 1994. nytimes.com/1994/05/09/nyregion/giuliani-broadens-crackdown-to
    -banish-all-illegal-vendors.html.
Hirsch, Joe. "NYOFCo to Close Its Doors," *Hunts Point Express* (NY), June 30, 2010. brie
    .hunter.cuny.edu/hpe/?p=3974.
Hondagneu-Sotelo, Pierrette. *Doméstica: Immigrant Workers Cleaning and Caring in
    the Shadows of Affluence*. Berkeley: University of California Press, 2001.
Hope, Bradley. "Changes Afoot on Manhattan's 'Last Frontier,'" *Sun* (NY), October 4,
    2007. nysun.com/real-estate/changes-afoot-on-manhattans-last-frontier/63938.
Horsford, Sonya Douglass. *Learning in a Burning House: Educational Inequality,
    Ideology, and (Dis)Integration*. New York: Teachers College Press, 2011.
Hu, Winnie. "Where a Little Girl Met Her Death, the Big Trucks Now Find a Hostile
    Welcome." *New York Times*, August 9, 1998. nytimes.com/1998/08/09/nyregion
    /neighborhood-reports-hunts-point-where-little-girl-met-her-death-big-trucks
    -now.html.
Hughes, Langston. "Black Misery." In *The Collected Works of Langston Hughes*, vol. 2,
    edited by Dianne Johnson, 171–76. Columbia: University of Missouri Press, 2003.
Hutchison, Beth. "Lesbian Blood Drives as Community-Building Activism in the 1980s."
    Journal of Lesbian Studies 19, no. 1 (2015): 117–28.
Hye, Alexandra. "From a 'Short Time' to 'A Way Out': Race, Militarism and Korean Sex
    Workers in New York." *Colorlines* 2, no. 2 (1999): 30.
Itagaki, Lynn. *Civil Racism: The 1992 Los Angeles Rebellion and the Crisis of Racial
    Burnout*. Minneapolis: University of Minnesota Press, 2016.
Iu, Maria. Letter. *Pacific Ties*. 31, no. 1 (2008): 3.
Jackson, Mandi Isaacs. "Harlem's Rent Strike and Rat War: Representation, Housing
    Access and Tenant Resistance in New York, 1958–1964." *American Studies* 47, no. 1
    (2006): 53–79.
Jacobs, Andrew. "Shuttered Clubs, Scrambled Lives." *New York Times*, October 11, 1998.
    nytimes.com/1998/10/11/nyregion/shuttered-clubs-scrambled-lives.html.

Jacoby, Russell. *Social Amnesia: A Critique of Conformist Psychology from Adler to Laing.* Boston: Beacon Press, 1975.

Jiang, Michelle. "Dozens of Tenants Rally for Protecting Their Rights," May 9, 2011, translated by Alex Peng. ourchinatown.org/2011/05/09/the-daily-five-may-9.

Jobin-Leeds, Greg, and AgitArte. *Why We Fight: Twenty-First Century Social Movements and the Activists That Are Transforming Our World.* New York: New Press, 2016.

Jung, Wooseok, Brayden G. King, and Sarah A. Soule. "Issue Bricolage: Explaining the Configuration of the Social Movement Sector, 1960–1995." *American Journal of Sociology* 120, no. 1 (2014): 187–225.

Kaalund, Valerie Ann. "Witness to Truth: Black Women Heeding the Call for Environmental Justice." In *New Perspectives on Environmental Justice: Gender, Sexuality, and Activism*, edited by Rachel Stein, 78–92. New Brunswick, NJ: Rutgers University Press, 2004.

Kalleberg, Arne L. *Good Jobs, Bad Jobs: The Rise of Polarized and Precarious Employment Systems in the United States, 1970s to 2000s.* New York: Russell Sage Foundation, 2011.

——. "Precarious Work, Insecure Workers: Employment Relations in Transition." *American Sociological Review* 74, no. 1 (2009): 1–22.

Kang, Miliann. "Manicuring Intimacies: Inequalities and Resistance in Nail Salon Work." In *Intimate Labors: Cultures, Technologies, and the Politics of Care*, edited by Eileen Boris and Rhacel Salazar Parreñas, 217–30. Stanford, CA: Stanford University Press, 2010.

Kao, Mary U., Eddie Kochiyama, Audee Kochiyama-Holman, and Ryan Kochiyama. "Tributes to Yuri Kochiyama." *Amerasia Journal* 40, no. 3 (2014): 1–32.

Kaplan, Temma. *Crazy for Democracy: Women in Grassroots Movements.* New York: Routledge, 1996.

Kappstatter, Bob. "Moms on the Line vs. Big Rig Traffic." *Daily News* (NY), July 29, 2002.

Karni, Annie. "NYC Crowned World's Business Capital." *Crain's New York Business*, June 4, 2013. crainsnewyork.com/article/20130604/ECONOMY/130609966.

Katz, Michael B. *The Undeserving Poor: America's Enduring Confrontation with Poverty.* 2nd ed. New York: Oxford University Press, 2013.

Keller, Bill. "The Bloomberg Legacy." *New York Times*, July 14, 2013, nytimes.com/2013/07/15/opinion/keller-the-bloomberg-legacy.html.

Kelley, Tina. "What Stinks? The Mourners Wore Hazmat Suits." *New York Times*, March 25, 2008. cityroom.blogs.nytimes.com/2008/03/25/what-stinks-the-mourners-wore-hazmat-suits.

Khan, Shazia. "Making Census of It: Chinatown No Longer Home To NYC's Largest Chinese Population." NY1 News, July 20, 2011.

Kim, Claire Jean. "Playing the Racial Trump Card: Asian Americans In Contemporary U.S. Politics." *Amerasia Journal* 26, no. 3 (2000): 35–65.

King, Martin Luther, Jr. "Where Do We Go from Here?" In *Say It Loud: Great Speeches on Civil Rights and African American Identity*, edited by Catherine Ellis and Stephen Drury Smith, 33–49. New York: New Press, 2010.

Klar, Malte, and Tim Kasser. "Some Benefits of Being an Activist: Measuring Activism and Its Role in Psychological Well-Being." *Political Psychology* 30, no. 5 (2009): 755–77.

Kneeland, Douglass E. "Reagan Urges Blacks to Look Past Labels and to Vote for Him." *New York Times*, August 6, 1980.

Kochiyama, Yuri. Preface to *Dragon Ladies: Asian American Feminists Breathe Fire,* ed. Sonia Shah, v–viii. Boston: South End Press, 1997.

Kurashige, Scott. "Pan-Ethnicity and Community Organizing: Asian Americans United's Campaign against Anti-Asian Violence." *Journal of Asian American Studies* 3, no. 2 (2000): 163–90.

Kvist, Elin, and Elin Petersen. "What Has Gender Equality Got to Do with It? An Analysis of Policy Debates Surrounding Domestic Services in the Welfare States of Spain and Sweden." *NORA: Nordic Journal of Feminist and Gender Research* 18, no. 3 (2010): 185–203.

La Ferla, Ruth. "General Tso's Shopping Spree." *New York Times*, September 17, 2008. nytimes.com/2008/09/18/fashion/18CHINATOWN.html.

Lambert, Susan, and Julia Henly. "Double Jeopardy: The Misfit between Welfare-to-Work Requirements and Job Realities." In *Work and the Welfare State: Street-Level Organizations and Workfare Politics*, edited by Evelyn Z. Brodkin and Gregory Marston, 69–84. Washington, DC: Georgetown University Press, 2013.

Lampe, David. "The Role of Gentrification in Central City Revitalization." *National Civic Review* 82, no. 4 (1993): 363–77.

Lawson, Ronald, and Stephen E. Barton, "Sex Roles in Social Movements: A Case Study of the Tenant Movement in New York City." *Signs* 6, no. 2 (1980): 230–47.

Lawson, Ronald, and Mark Naison, eds. *The Tenant Movement in New York City: 1904–1984*. Piscataway, NJ: Rutgers University Press, 1986.

Lee, Chisun. "Asian Power: Keeping Up the Struggle Against Police Violence." *Village Voice* (NY), March 21, 2000, 27.

———. "Domestic Disturbance: The Help Set out to Help Themselves." *Village Voice* (NY), March 12, 2002.

Lee, Erika. "Immigrants and Immigration Law: A State of the Field Assessment." *Journal of American Ethnic History* 18, no. 4 (1999): 85–114.

———. "The 'Yellow Peril' and Asian Exclusion in the Americas." *Pacific Historical Review* 76, no. 4 (2007): 537–62.

Lee, Felicia R. "Cut, Baste, Stitch, Sing!" *New York Times*, June 21, 2011. nytimes.com/2011/06/22/theater/furee-in-pins-needles-at-irondale-center.html.

Lee, Jennifer 8. "Harassment Is Focus of Chinatown Tenants' Suit." *New York Times*, February 18, 2009. cityroom.blogs.nytimes.com/2009/02/18/harassment-is-focus-of-chinatown-tenants-suit.

Leonhardt, David. "Our Broken Economy, in One Simple Chart." *New York Times*, August 7, 2017. nytimes.com/interactive/2017/08/07/opinion/leonhardt-income-inequality.html.

Li, Wei. "Beyond Chinatown, beyond Enclave: Reconceptualizing Contemporary Chinese Settlements in the United States." *GeoJournal* 64, no. 1 (2005): 31–40.

Lien, Pei-Te. *Making of Asian America: Through Political Participation*. Philadelphia: Temple University Press, 2010.

Lilla, Mark. *The Once and Future Liberal: After Identity Politics*. New York: Harper, 2017.

Limoncelli, Stephanie A. "The Trouble with Trafficking: Conceptualizing Women's Sexual Labor and Economic Human Rights." *Women Studies International Forum* 32, no. 4 (2009): 261–69.

Liu, Michael, and Kim Geron. "Changing Neighborhood: Ethnic Enclaves and the Struggle for Social Justice." *Social Justice* 35, no. 2 (2008): 18–35.

Liu, Michael, Kim Geron, and Tracy Lai. *The Snake Dance of Asian American Activism*. Lanham, MD: Lexington Books, 2008.

Liu, Mini. "Dangerous Upsurge in Immigrant Scapegoating." CAAAV *Voice* (1988): 3–4.

Lobbia, J. A. "Civics Lesson: Chinatown Youths Learn Tenant Activism," *Village Voice* (NY), August 1, 2000.

López, Ian Haney. *Dog Whistle Politics: How Coded Racial Appeals Have Reinvented Racism and Wrecked the Middle Class*. Oxford: Oxford University Press, 2015.

Lorde, Audre. 1978. "A Litany for Survival." In *The Black Unicorn*, 31–32. New York: Norton.

Lowe, Lisa. *Immigrant Acts: On Asian American Cultural Politics*. Durham, NC: Duke University Press, 1996.

Lugones, María C., and Elizabeth V. Spelman. "Have We Got a Theory for You! Feminist Theory, Cultural Imperialism, and the Demand for 'The Woman's Voice.'" *Women's Studies International Forum* 6, no. 6 (1983): 573–81.

Luibhéid, Eithne. *Entry Denied: Controlling Sexuality at the Border*. Minneapolis: University of Minnesota, 2002.

Luxemburg, Rosa. "The Russian Revolution." In *The Rosa Luxemburg Reader*, edited by Peter Hudis and Kevin B. Anderson, 281–311. New York: Monthly Review Press, 2004.

Mackenzie, Victoria. "The Sweet Smell of Victory; MOM Celebrates Victory and Keeps on Moving." *Bronx Free Press* 1, no. 21 (2010).

Mainland, Alexis, Manny Fernandez, and Christian Hansen. "Failed Elevators, Frustrated Residents," *New York Times*, November 15, 2008. nytimes.com /interactive/2008/11/15/nyregion/16elevators-wagner/index.html.

Martinez, Jose. "Crash Shatters 2 Families: Bronx Moms Had Put Their Lives in Order." *Daily News* (NY), July 22, 2001. "Hunts Pt. Group Has Traffic Plan." *Daily News* (NY), April 25, 2001.

Martins, Chris. "2017 No. 1s: Cardi B on Her Rise to Hot 100 History." *Billboard*. December 21, 2017. billboard.com/articles/events/year-in-music-2017/8071047 /cardi-b-hot-100-history-interview-no-1s-2017.

Matsubara, Hiroyuki. "Stratified Whiteness and Sexualized Chinese Immigrants in San Francisco: The Report of the California Special Committee on Chinese Immigration in 1876." *American Studies International*, 41, no. 3 (2003): 32–59.

McCarty, Maggie. *Introduction to Public Housing*. Washington, DC: Congressional Research Service, 2014. www.fas.org/sgp/crs/misc/R41654.pdf.

McClain, Dani. "Former Residents of New Orleans's Demolished Housing Projects Tell Their Stories." *Nation*, August 28, 2015. thenation.com/article/former-residents-of -new-orleans-demolished-housing-projects-tell-their-stories.

McDonald, Avril. "Audre Lorde Nixes Lambda Award over *Miss Saigon* Flap." *OutWeek*, March 27, 1991, 14–16.

————. "Gay Asians Dispute Use of *Miss Saigon*." *OutWeek*, February 27, 1991, 14–15.

McKinley, James C., Jr. "The Giuliani Budget: The Overview; Giuliani's Budget Proposes Cuts for Spending and Work Force." *New York Times*, May 11, 1994. nytimes.com/1994/05/11/nyregion/giuliani-budget-overview-giuliani-s-budget-proposes-cuts-for-spending-work-force.html.

Mediratta, Kavitha, and Jessica Karp. *Parent Power and Urban School Reform: The Story of Mothers on the Move*. New York: New York University Institute for Education and Social Policy, 2003. steinhardt.nyu.edu/scmsAdmin/media/users/ggg5/Parent_Power_and_Urban_School_Reform_-_Mediratta_Karp_Nov_2003.pdf.

Mercado, Andrea Cristina, and Ai-Jen Poo. *Domestic Workers Organizing in the United States*. Toronto: Association for Women's Rights in Development, 2008.

Meyer, David. "Sheridan Expressway Removal Gets $97 Million Boost in State Budget." Streets Blog NYC, April 5, 2016. nyc.streetsblog.org/2016/04/05/sheridan-expressway-removal-gets-97-million-boost-in-state-budget.

Middaugh, Laine. "Lessons from the 'Unorganizable' Domestic Workers Organizing." *Kennedy School Review* 12, no. 1 (2012): 12–13.

Moon, Katharine. *Sex among Allies: Military Prostitution in U.S.-Korea Relations*. New York: Columbia University Press, 1997.

Moore, Larkin M. 2007. "Stranded Again: The Inadequacy of Federal Plans to Rebuild an Affordable New Orleans after Hurricane Katrina." *Boston College Third World Law Journal* 27, no. 1 (2007): 227–62.

Moraga, Cherríe Moraga, and Gloria Anzaldúa, eds. *This Bridge Called My Back: Writings by Radical Women of Color*. Boston: Kitchen Table Press, 1981.

MOM [Mothers on the Move]. "City Owes Mott Haven Tenants Jobs, Advocates Contend." *On the Move/En Movimiento*, May 6, 2011, mothersonthemove.blogspot.com/2011/05/city-owes-mott-haven-tenants-jobs.html.

————. "Report on NYCHA Green Jobs Meeting." *On the Move/En Movimiento*, October 17, 2010. mothersonthemove.blogspot.com/2010/10/report-on-nycha-green-jobs-meeting.html

————. "South Bronx Bus Tour Raising a Stink in Hunts Point." New York City Independent Media Center, June 8, 2007. nyc.indymedia.org/or/2007/06/87129.html.

MOM [Mothers on the Move] and Urban Justice Center. *Change Starts with Us: A Grassroots Vision for the Development of the South Bronx*. New York: Urban Justice, 2010. cdp.urbanjustice.org/sites/default/files/ChangsStartswithUs_03mar10.pdf.

Moynihan, Colin. "A Turning Point for the East Village, 20 Years Later." *New York Times*, June 3, 2011. cityroom.blogs.nytimes.com/2011/06/03/a-turning-point-for-the-east-village-20-years-later.

Muñoz, José Esteban. *Disidentifications: Queers of Color and the Performance of Politics*. Minneapolis: University of Minnesota Press, 1999.

Murphy, Alexander K., and Sudir Alladi Venkatesh. "Vice Careers: The Changing Contours of Sex Work in New York City." *Qualitative Sociology* 29, no. 2 (2006): 129–54.

NAACP Legal Defense and Educational Fund. "Stop and Frisks Lead To More Fallout For

Public Housing Residents." *PR Newswire*, April 10, 2013. www.prnewswire.com
/news-releases/stop—frisks-lead-to-more-fallout-for-public-housing-residents
-202340811.html.

Naples, Nancy A. *Grassroots Warriors: Activist Mothering, Community Work, and the
War on Poverty*. New York: Routledge, 1998.

Nash, Jennifer C. "Re-Thinking Intersectionality." *Feminist Review* 89, no. 1 (2008):
1–15.

Nash, Kate. "The Feminist Critique of Liberal Individualism as Masculinist." *Journal of
Political Ideologies* 2, no. 1 (1997): 13.

Navarro, Mireya. "227,000 Names on List Vie for Rare Vacancies in City's Public
Housing," *New York Times*, July 23, 2013. www.nytimes.com/2013/07/24/nyregion
/for-many-seeking-public-housing-the-wait-can-be-endless.html.

NBC News. "Race 'Doesn't Matter': Reactions to Officer Liang's Indictment." *NBC News*,
February 11, 2015. nbcnews.com/news/asian-america/race-doesnt-matter
-reactions-officer-liangs-indictment-n304431.

Nelson, Maggie. *The Argonauts*. Minneapolis, MN: Gray Wolf Press, 2015.

New York City Department of Planning. *NYC2010 Results from the US Census:
Population Growth and Race/Hispanic Composition*. New York: Department of
Planning, 2011. www1.nyc.gov/assets/planning/download/pdf/data-maps/nyc
-population/census2010/pgrhc.pdf.

NYCHA [New York City Housing Authority]. NYCHA *2018 Fact Sheet*. New York: NYCHA,
2018. www1.nyc.gov/assets/nycha/downloads/pdf/NYCHA-Fact-Sheet_2018
_Final.pdf.

New York Times. "Settlement Reached in Police Shooting Suit." *New York Times*, March
13, 1996. nytimes.com/1996/03/13/nyregion/settlement-reached-in-police
-shooting-suit.html.

Nguyen, Mai Thi, Victoria Basolo, and Abhishek Tiwari. "Opposition to Affordable
Housing in the USA: Debate Framing and the Responses of Local Actors." *Housing,
Theory, and Society* 30, no. 2 (2013): 107–30.

Nguyen, Sahra V. "NBC Asian America Presents: Deported." NBC Asian America, March
17, 2017. nbcnews.com/news/asian-america/nbc-asian-america-presents
-deported-n734051.

Nicholson, Andre. "The Classification of Black Celebrity Women in Cyberspace."
Black Women and Popular Culture : The Conversation Continues, edited by Adria Y.
Goldman et al., 273–90. Lanham, MD: Lexington Books, 2014.

Nossiter, Adam. "Asthma Common and on Rise In the Crowded South Bronx." *New York
Times*, September 5, 1995. nytimes.com/1995/09/05/us/asthma-common-and-on
-rise-in-the-crowded-south-bronx.html.

NY1 News. "Activists Hold 'Toxic Bus Tour' of South Bronx." *NY1 News*, August 17, 2008.

NYC Opportunity. *New York City Government Poverty Measure 2005–2015: An Annual
Report from the Office of the Mayor*. New York: Mayor's Office of Operations, 2017.

Obias, Leah. "Organizing Domestic Workers: The National Domestic Workers Alliance."
S&F Online 8, no. 1 (2009).

Office of the Attorney General New York. "Attorney General Cuomo Sues South Bronx

Fertilizer Company to End Noxious Odors That Threaten Health and Well-Being of Hunts Points Residents." Media Center, February 5, 2009.

———. "Spitzer Announces New Board for Banana Kelly Community Improvement Association." Media Center, November 7, 2002.

Okamoto, Dina G. "Institutional Panethnicity: Boundary Formation in Asian-American Organizing." *Social Forces* 85, no. 1 (2006): 1–25.

———. "Toward a Theory of Panethnicity: Explaining Asian American Collective Action." *American Sociological Review* 68, no. 6 (2003): 811–42.

Olmeda, Rafael A. "Walk on the Wild Side: A Message to Drivers." *Daily News* (NY), September 24, 1998.

Omatsu, Glenn. "Kazu Iijima, 1918–2007." *Amerasia Journal* 33, no. 3 (2007): vi–ix.

Orleck, Annelise. *Storming Caesar's Palace: How Black Mothers Fought Their Own War on Poverty.* Boston: Beacon Press, 2005.

Orleck, Annelise, and Lisa Gayle Hazirjian, eds. *The War on Poverty: A New Grassroots History, 1964–1980.* Athens, GA: University of Georgia Press, 2011.

Osajima, Keith. "Asian Americans as the Model Minority: An Analysis of the Popular Press Image in the 1960s and 1980s." In *Reflections on Shattered Windows: Promises and Prospects for Asian American Studies,* edited by Gary Okihiro, John M. Liu, Arthur A. Hansen, and Shirley Hune, 165–74. Pullman: Washington State University Press, 1988.

Oster, Marcy. "On Day of Women's March, Sarsour Rejects Farrakhan's Anti-Semitism and Defends BDS." *Jewish Telegraphic Agency,* January 20, 2019. www.jta.org/2019 /01/20/united-states/sarsour-at-womens-march-touts-bds-hours-after-rejecting -farrakhans-anti-semitism.

Outweek. "On Missing *Miss Saigon.*" *OutWeek,* March 27, 1991, 4.

Pace, Eric. "Astin Jacobo, 73, Unofficial Mayor of a Bronx Neighborhood." *New York Times,* March 30, 2002. www.nytimes.com/2002/03/30/nyregion/astin-jacobo-73 -unofficial-mayor-of-a-bronx-neighborhood.html.

Parreñas, Rhacel Salazar. *The Force of Domesticity: Filipina Migrants and Globalization.* New York: New York University Press, 2008.

Perry, Leah. *The Cultural Politics of U.S. Immigration: Gender, Race, and Media.* New York: New York University Press, 2016.

Polletta, Francesca. *Freedom Is an Endless Meeting.* University of Chicago Press, 2002.

Poo, Ai-jen. "A Twentieth-First Century Organizing Model: Lessons from the New York Domestic Workers Bill of Rights Campaign." *New Labor Forum* 20, no. 1 (Winter 2011): 50–55.

Portlock, Arah. "Asthma Plagues South Bronx Neighborhood." *Washington Square News,* December 9, 2005.

Powell, Michael. "Her Chinatown Home is 'Underperforming.'" *New York Times,* August 15, 2011. nytimes.com/2011/08/16/nyregion/chinatown-woman-fights-real-estate -firms-pressure.html.

Puar, Jasbir K. "'I would rather be a cyborg than a goddess': Becoming-Intersectional in Assemblage Theory." *philoSOPHIA* 2, no. 1 (2012): 49–66. eipcp.net/transversal/0811 /puar/en.

———. *Terrorist Assemblages: Homonationalism in Queer Times*. Durham, NC: Duke University Press, 2007.

Rand, Erica. *The Ellis Island Snow Globe*. Durham, NC: Duke University Press, 2005.

Rankin, Kenrya. "Asian-American Coalition Issues Powerful Statement about Peter Liang's Sentence of Community Service." *Colorlines*, April 20, 2016. colorlines.com /articles/asian-american-coalition-issues-powerful-statement-about-peter-liangs -sentence-community.

Ransby, Barbara. *Ella Baker and the Black Freedom Movement*. Chapel Hill: University of North Carolina Press, 2005.

Rivas, Jorge. "NYC's Chinatown Devastated after Sandy, Advocates Say Race to Blame." *Colorlines*. November 2, 2012. www.colorlines.com/articles/nycs-chinatown -devastated-after-sandy-advocates-say-race-blame.

Rivera, Maritza Quiñones. "From Triguenita to Afro-Puerto Rican: Intersections of the Racialized, Gendered, and Sexualized Body in Puerto Rico and the US Mainland." *Meridians* 7, no. 1 (2006): 162–82.

Roberts, Sam. "No Longer Majority Black, Harlem is in Transition." *New York Times*, January 5, 2010. www.nytimes.com/2010/01/06/nyregion/06harlem.html.

———. "Poverty Rate Is up in New York City, and Income Gap Is Wide, Census Data Show." *New York Times*, September 19, 2013. nytimes.com/2013/09/19/nyregion /poverty-rate-in-city-rises-to-21-2.html.

Robinson, Greg. "Nisei in Gotham: The JACD and Japanese Americans in 1940s New York." *Prospects: An Annual of American Cultural Studies* 30 (2005): 581–95.

Rodney, Seph. "Activists Protest Swizz Beatz's Art Fair in the Bronx." Hyperallergic, August 16, 2016. hyperallergic.com/317371/activists-protest-swizz-beatzs-art-fair-in -the-bronx.

Rotramel, Ariella. "'This is like family': Activist-Survivor Histories and Motherwork." In *U.S. Women's History: Untangling the Threads of Sisterhood*, edited by Leslie Brown, Anne Valk and Jacqueline Castledine, 49–62. Piscataway, NJ: Rutgers University Press, 2017.

———. "We Make the Spring Rolls, They Make Their Own Rules: Filipina Domestic Workers' Fight for Labor Rights in New York City and Los Angeles." *AAPI Nexus Journal: Policy, Practice and Community* 10, no. 2 (2012): 77–98.

Rutenberg, James. "Big Trucks Rock and Roll Over City DOT Eying Reroute Plan." *Daily News* (NY), March 2, 1999.

Sampaio, Anna. "Transnational Feminisms in a New Global Matrix." *International Feminist Journal of Politics* 6, no. 2 (2004): 181–206.

Samuel, Raphael. "History and Theory." In *People's History and Socialist Theory*, edited by Raphael Samuel, xl–lvi. New York: Routledge, 2016.

Sandoval, Chela. *Methodology of the Oppressed*. Minneapolis: University of Minnesota Press, 2000.

Santiago, Katherine. "New York City Tenants Rally for Better Housing," May 2, 2008. katherinesantiago.wordpress.com/2008/05/02/new-york-city-tenants-rally-for -better-housing.

Sassen, Saskia. "Economic Cleansing: Failure Dressed in Fine Clothes." *Social Research* 83, no. 3 (2016): 673–87.

———. "The Global City: Introducing a Concept." *Brown Journal of World Affairs* 11, no. 2 (2005): 27–43.

Schwartzman, Lisa H. *Challenging Liberalism: Feminism As Political Critique.* University Park: Penn State University Press, 2006.

Sen, Rinku. *Stir It up: Lessons in Community Organizing and Advocacy.* San Francisco: Jossey-Bass, 2003.

Serrano, Jose E. "The Serrano Report" July 11, 2008.

Service Employees International Union. "Residents, City Officials Concerned about Synagro Sludge to Travel to DC to Appeal to Carlyle's Rubenstein to Have Third-Party Test Sludge," Reuters, April 29, 2008.

Shah, Hina B., and Seville, Marci. "Domestic Worker Organizing: Building a Contemporary Movement for Dignity and Power." *Albany Law Review* 75, no. 1 (2012): 413–47.

Shapiro, Julie. "Displaced Tenants Get Little Help Due to Landlord Violations." *Downtown Express* (NY), January 2009, www.thevillager.com/2009/01/displaced -tenants-get-little-help-due-to-landlord-violations.

Shima, Alan. "The Differential of Appearance: Asian American Cultural Studies," *Journal of American Studies* 32, no. 2 (1998): 283–93.

Shimizu, Celine Parreñas. "The Bind of Representation: Performing and Consuming Hypersexuality in 'Miss Saigon.'" *Theatre Journal* 57, no. 2 (2005): 247–65.

Shu, Yuan. "Reading the Kung Fu Film in an American Context: From Bruce Lee to Jackie Chan." *Journal of Popular Film and Television* 31, no. 2 (2003): 50–59.

Silliman, Jael, Marlene Gerber Fried, Loretta Ross, and Elena Guiterrez. *Undivided Rights: Women of Color Organizing for Reproductive Justice.* Boston: South End Press, 2005.

Sinclair, Betsy, Margaret McConnell, and Melissa R. Michelson. "Local Canvassing: The Efficacy of Grassroots Voter Mobilization." *Political Communication* 30, no. 1 (2013): 42–57.

Small, Andrew. "Gentrification of Gotham." CityLab, April 28, 2017.

Smith, Greg B. "NYCHA Chairman John Rhea Booed Over Misuse of Funds, Luxury High-Rise Plan." *Daily News* (NY), July 24, 2013. nydailynews.com/new-york/nycha -chairman-john-rhea-booed-misuse-funds-article-1.1408240.

———. "NYCHA Tenants, Lawmakers to Protest Leasing Public Housing Land for Private Development." *Daily News* (NY), June 10, 2013. nydailynews.com/new -york/nycha-leasing-plan-face-protest-tuesday-article-1.1368635.

Smith, Neil. "New City, New Frontier: The Lower East Side as Wild, Wild West." In *Variations on a Theme Park: The New American City and the End of Public Space,* edited by Michael Sorkin, 61–93. New York: Noonday Press, 1992.

Smith, Peggie R. "Organizing the Unorganizable: Private Paid Household Workers and Approaches to Employee Representation." *North Carolina Law Review* 79, no. 1 (2000): 45–110.

Solis, Hilda L. "Remarks by Hilda L. Solis, Secretary of Labor, National Domestic Worker Alliance Inaugural Care Congress." United States Department of Labor. July 12, 2011. votesmart.org/public-statement/622854/remarks-by-hilda-l-solis

-secretary-of-labor-at-national-domestic-worker-alliance-inaugural-care
-congress#.XJNvsFNKiCQ.

Spade, Dean. "Now Is the Time for 'Nobodies': Dean Spade on Mutual Aid and
Resistance in the Trump Era." Alternet. January 9, 2017. deanspade.net/2017/01/09
/now-is-the-time-for-nobodies-dean-spade-on-mutual-aid-and-resistance-in-the
-trump-era.

Stack, Liam. "Protest Against Fox Correspondent Accused of Racism for Chinatown
Interviews." New York Times, October 6, 2016. nytimes.com/2016/10/07/business
/media/fox-reporter-accused-of-racism-for-chinatown-interviews-on-trump
-clinton-and-china.html.

Starnes, Todd. "CNN, MSNBC Using Florida Teens as Anti-Trump Propaganda Pawns,"
Fox News, February 20, 2018.foxnews.com/opinion/2018/02/20/cnn-msnbc-using
-florida-teens-as-anti-trump-propaganda-pawns.html.

Steinhauser, Gabrielle. "Ladies and Gentlemen, the Bronx Is Choking!" Straus Media,
May 14, 2008. nypress.com/ladies-and-gentlementhe-bronx-is-choking.

Steward, Brenda. "'Working for My Benefits.' Brenda Steward Describes the Work
Experience Program (WEP) in New York City." Interviewed by Janine Jackson.
History Matters, 1996. historymatters.gmu.edu/d/7031.

StreetEasy. "Rents Have Increased Twice as Fast as Wages in New York City Since 2010."
PR Newswire, August 16, 2017. www.prnewswire.com/news-releases/rents-have
-increased-twice-as-fast-as-wages-in-new-york-city-since-2010–300505028
.html.

SAMHSA [Substance Abuse and Mental Health Services Administration]. "Results from
the 2015 National Survey on Drug Use and Health: Detailed Tables," September 8,
2016, www.samhsa.gov/data/sites/default/files/NSDUH-DetTabs
-2015/NSDUH-DetTabs-2015/NSDUH-DetTabs-2015.pdf.

Sze, Julie. Noxious New York: The Racial Politics of Urban Health and Environmental
Justice. Cambridge, MA: MIT Press, 2007.

Tang, Eric. Unsettled: Cambodian Refugees in the New York City Hyperghetto.
Philadelphia: Temple University Press, 2015.

Taylor, Keeanga-Yamahtta. From #BlackLivesMatter to Black Liberation. Chicago:
Haymarket Books, 2016.

———. Introduction. In How We Get Free: Black Feminism and the Combahee River
Collective, edited by Keeanga-Yamahtta Taylor, 1–14. Chicago: Haymarket Books,
2017.

Tchen, John Kuo Wei. New York before Chinatown: Orientalism and the Shaping of
American Culture, 1776–1882. Baltimore, MD: Johns Hopkins University Press, 1999.

Thompson, Becky. "Multiracial Feminism: Recasting the Chronology of Second Wave
Feminism." Feminist Studies 28, no. 2 (2002): 337–60.

Tracy, Thomas, et al. "NYPD Cop Peter Liang Guilty in Fatal Shooting of Akai Gurley."
Daily News (NY), February 12, 2016. nydailynews.com/new-york/nyc-crime/nypd
-peter-liang-guilty-fatal-shooting-akai-gurley-article-1.2528827.

Transportation Alternatives. "DOT Faces Rough Treatment in the Bronx."
Transportation Alternatives Magazine 5, no. 1 (1999): 14.

Tri-State Transportation Campaign. "Bronx Neighborhood Wants NYC DOT's Word on Truck Safety." Tri-State Transportation Campaign, December 11, 1998.

Trigg, Mary, and Alison Bernstein, eds. *Junctures in Women's Leadership: Social Movements*. Piscataway, NJ: Rutgers University Press, 2016.

Tsui, Bonnie. "City within a City." In *American Chinatown: A People's History of Five Neighborhoods*, 61–76. New York: Free Press, 2009.

Uhl-Bien, Mary. "Relational Leadership Theory: Exploring the Social Processes of Leadership and Organizing." *Leadership Quarterly* 17, no. 4 (2006): 654–76.

Union Review. "On May 1 Teamster Local 237 Held a Spirited Rally to Raise Awareness to the NYCHA Budget Cuts." Union Review, May 13, 2008. archive.unionreview.com /may-1-teamster-local-237-held-sprited-rally-raise-awareness-nycha-budget-cuts.

U.S. Census Bureau. "21.3 Percent of U.S. Population Participates in Government Assistance Programs Each Month." U.S. Department of Commerce, May 28, 2015. census.gov/newsroom/press-releases/2015/cb15-97.html.

Venugopal, Arun. "Sailing Round Manhattan on the Sludge Boat." WNYC News, April 1, 2009. wnyc.org/story/74867-sailing-round-manhattan-on-the-sludge-boat.

Vespa, Jonathan, Jamie M. Lewis, and Rose M. Kreider. *America's Families and Living Arrangements: 2012*. Washington: DC: United States Census Bureau, 2013. census .gov/prod/2013pubs/p20-570.pdf.

Villano, Vincent, and Sondra Youdelman. *Democracy (In)action: How HUD, NYCHA, and Official Structures Undermine Resident Participation in New York Public Housing*. New York: Community Voices Heard, 2010.

Volscho, Thomas W., and Nathan J. Kelly. "The Rise of the Super-Rich: Power Resources, Taxes, Financial Markets, and the Dynamics of the Top 1 Percent, 1949 to 2008." *American Sociological Review* 77, no. 5 (2012): 679–99.

von Hassell, Malve. "Names of Hate, Names of Love: Contested Space and the Formation of Identity on Manhattan's Lower East Side." *Dialectical Anthropology* 23, no. 4 (1998): 375–413.

Wade, Lisa. "Loretta Ross on the Phrase "Women of Color." *Sociological Images*, March 26, 2011. thesocietypages.org/socimages/2011/03/26/loreta-ross-on-the-phrase -women-of-color

Waldman, Amy. "Trash Giant Skirts Conditions Set for Bronx Station, Critics Say." *New York Times*, August 24, 1999. nytimes.com/1999/08/24/nyregion/trash-giant-skirts -conditions-set-for-bronx-station-critics-say.html.

Walters, Suzanna Danuta. "In Defense of Identity Politics." *Signs: Journal of Women in Culture and Society*, Fall 2017. signsjournal.org/currents-identity-politics/walters.

Wang, Esther. "The Pleasures of Protest: Taking on Gentrification in Chinatown." Longreads, August 2016. longreads.com/2016/09/06/the-pleasures-of-protest -taking-on-gentrification-in-chinatown.

Warren, Mathew. "Hunts Point Residents Sue over a Smell." *New York Times*, July 20, 2008. nytimes.com/2008/07/10/nyregion/10bronx.html?_r=1.

Wei, William. *The Asian American Movement*. Philadelphia: Temple University Press, 1993.

White, Deborah Grey. *Too Heavy a Load: Black Women in Defense of Themselves, 1894–1994*. New York: Norton, 1999.

White, Stuart M. "NYCHA Owes Tenants Jobs, Advocates Contend." *Hunts Point Express* (NY), April 29, 2011. http://brie.hunter.cuny.edu/hpe/?p=6024.

Wial, Howard. "Where the 1% Live." CityLab, October 31, 2011. citylab.com/life/2011/10/where-one-percent-live/393.

WNYC. "New York Remade: The Bloomberg Years," July–December 2013. www.wnyc.org/series/new-york-remade-bloomberg-years.

Women of Color Network. *Women of Color Network Facts and Stats: Domestic Violence in Communities of Color.* Harrisburg, PA: Women of Color Network, 2006. www.doj.state.or.us/wp-content/uploads/2017/08/women_of_color_network_facts_domestic_violence_2006.pdf.

Wong, Julia Carrie. "'Scapegoated?' The Police Killing That Left Asian Americans Angry—and Divided." *Guardian*, April 18, 2016. theguardian.com/world/2016/apr/18/peter-liang-akai-gurley-killing-asian-american-response.

World Bank. "Inside the Household: Poor Children, Women, and Men." In *Poverty and Shared Prosperity 2018*, 125–49. New York: World Bank, 2018.

Wright, Melissa W. "Urban Geography Plenary Lecture—Femicide, Mother-Activism, and the Geography of Protest in Northern Mexico." *Urban Geography* 28, no. 5 (2007): 401–25.

Wynn, Terry. "South Bronx Rises Out of the Ashes." NBC News, January 17, 2005. nbcnews.com/id/6807914/ns/us_news/t/south-bronx-rises-out-ashes/#.U_NoOrxdXRY.

Yin, Stephanie. "In a Black-and-White America, Asians Struggle to Fit In." *Complex*, March 18, 2016. complex.com/life/2016/03/asian-america-race.

Yoshikawa, Yoko. "The Heat Is on *Miss Saigon* Coalition: Organizing Across Race and Sexuality." In *Q&A: Queer in Asia America*, edited by David L. Eng and Alice Y. Hom, 41–56. Philadelphia: Temple University Press, 1998.

Young, Iris Marion. "The Five Faces of Oppression." In *Justice and the Politics of Difference*, 39–65. Princeton, NJ: Princeton University Press, 1990.

Yu, Phil. "Remember Vincent Chin." Angry Asian Man, June 20, 2011. blog.angryasianman.com/2011/06/remember-vincent-chin-vigil-june-23.html.

Yukich, Grace. "Constructing the Model Immigrant: Movement Strategy and Immigrant Deservingness in the New Sanctuary Movement." *Social Problems* 60, no. 3 (2013): 302–20.

Zimmer, Amy. "Chinatown: The Last Frontier." *Brooklyn Rail*, October 2004. brooklynrail.org/2004/10/streets/chinatown-the-last-frontier.

——. "Dividing Line between Upper East Side and Harlem Blurring." DNA Info, New York Public Radio, August 4, 2011. dnainfo.com/new-york/20110804/upper-east-side/dividing-line-between-upper-east-side-harlem-blurring.

Zukin, Sharon. *Naked City: The Death and Life of Authentic Urban Places.* New York: Oxford University Press, 2010.

INDEX

www.ingramcontent.com/pod-product-compliance
Lightning Source LLC
Chambersburg PA
CBHW010113270326
41926CB00024B/4510